AF412615

TRUTH OF BEAUTY

Truth Of Beauty

The Path to Uncovering the Beautiful You

by

Curtis Quinntin Phelps

with Max S. Gordon

Martin & Davis Publishing

New York

First Published in the United States by
Martin & Davis Publishing, New York

Truth of Beauty: The Path to Uncovering the Beautiful You

Printed in the United States of America

Book design by Andy Carpenter

Photography by JoAnne Noel Higgins

Names: Phelps, Curtis Quinntin author, Gordon, Max S. author

Some of the personal stories included in this book are composites
of several individuals.

Description: First Edition

Subjects: Self-Actualization, Self-Help, Transformation

First Edition September 2021

10 9 8 7 6 5 4 3 2 1

ACKNOWLEDGEMENTS

I'd like to thank the following people for their
loving contribution to the completion of this book.

Alethea Gordon, Rufus Müller,
Marilyn Phelps-Sandefer, Diane Wilson,
Robin Joy Riggsbee, Liav Abraham,
Lisa Blair, Heide Banks,
Jillian Veran, Jamal Swift,
James R. Dyke and
Maria Romano-Bates

This book is dedicated to my mother and first teacher in beauty, Cora Lee Phelps

…and to the beauty that exists in all of us.

TABLE OF CONTENTS

*"Beauty is truth, truth beauty—
that is all ye know on earth, and
all ye need to know."*
John Keats

TRUTH OF BEAUTY

Introduction

All beauty begins with a relationship with self.

It's been said many times about personal transformation, and it's true: an appreciation of the self is the most important relationship we can have. Being and living in beauty is not about being narcissistic or caring only about ourselves. It's about taking the time to get to know yourself so that you have a better understanding not only of who you are, but of what you want, and what you are putting forward into the world. Beauty, in other words, begins with greater self-awareness.

I believe that everyone wants to be in the world as a happier, more loving individual, if for no one else, at least for themselves. We all want to live in that beautiful place that often we only dream of; but we may not know how, or we are overwhelmed by our conditioning in life.

Conditioning here is defined by the habits we develop or have been taught in order to protect ourselves from the experience of pain or humiliation. They are precisely named because they are "conditional". In other words, when we are acting from our conditioning, we look to see what is going on "out there" in the world and then we adjust ourselves accordingly in order to get what we think we want. This is the opposite of standing with confidence in our power and fulfilling our purpose in the world.

When you are in your truth, every step you take and every choice you make each day means that you are more aligned with self.

Unfortunately, too many of us respond to life from that place of limitation, making choices based on what someone else says we are "supposed" to do, or who we were told we were "supposed" to be. The more aware you are of the effect these unwanted conditions have on your life and choices, the better you are able to leave them behind, giving the world your full beauty and attention. Imagine what your life would look like free of the conditions you don't want, a life where all of your attention goes to your being happy and living in your most beautiful world, fulfilling your life's purpose every day. Now imagine the world where every person is beautiful in her or his own right, experiencing beauty from a personal and unique place of joy.

I began my career in the beauty business, becoming a hairstylist and then a make-up artist, spokesperson and personal shopper. Unlike what I'd imagined when I first started out, the beauty and fashion world too often seemed vain, narcissistic, conniving, and even, at times, backstabbing. It was odd to me how people were using what appeared to be beauty in such unattractive ways – it felt downright ugly and puzzled me terribly. What I learned is that physical beauty usually gets attention and sometimes power. But when it is used to hurt, or to damage or disempower, I believe we've lost touch with what beauty actually is. As someone in the industry, I found that I needed to return to the essence of beauty; to "save" beauty. I wanted to explore what it means to be beautiful in truth, how beauty actually functions in the world, and to remember the reason people look for beauty in their lives; the reason people want to be beautiful.

This book is the result of that exploration. My philosophy is that we all want to live in our most beautiful world. Being in your beautiful world feels good, feels "attractive", and creates what you want in life. We may wish to follow "the Joneses" and the latest fashion trends, but while that can be fun and instructive, it only has validity when it helps inform what we want for ourselves in our own life. Beauty, as I see it, isn't truly personal until we define it for ourselves and appreciate how it is expressed in our own lives. To be truly beautiful, you have to "discover" the beauty in you first. When I was able to locate what beauty meant to me personally, I was able to target it more clearly for my clients.

I have found that with teaching Truth of Beauty, it has been helpful to share my experience of working with others. My hope is that, through their experiences, you will see something that mirrors your own. While I have changed a few details and combined a few stories to respect each client's privacy, please know that the emotional truth of each profile remains, and I am grateful to them for allowing me to use their stories as an inspiration for others.

What I have discovered from my years of consulting with clients is that true beauty, the beauty we will explore in these pages, can't be lost or taken away from you. It isn't found on a shelf in a drug store or on the rack in a boutique. It is your birthright, your purpose for being here, the beautiful gift that you bring to the world. When you discover, or rather "uncover" that part of you – uncover, because it has always been there, even if you've forgotten it or don't quite know how to access it – then you will know what true beauty means.

We've all passed someone on the street who was radiating an unmistakably beautiful energy. When you are that person, everyone around you begins to feel that energy; it's infectious. This is why discovering the person you really are and your relationship with self becomes the ultimate tool in your being beautiful inside and out.

Truth of Beauty is the relationship with yourself that allows you to go into the world and relate to society from a place of wholeness. Our whole world changes when we radiate who we actually are, as opposed to expecting others to validate us. This is not about "change" as it is usually defined, but rather a process of discovery – an uncovering of who you actually are, who you've always been or may have a fear of revealing.

The truth of beauty, ultimately, is you.

My own personal relationship with beauty began with the visual. Early in my life I was very attracted to physical beauty. I was so attracted to it, in fact, that I noticed myself staring in the mirror far more than I wanted to, always concerned about my own appearance. Everything was about "the look". That led me to paying attention to hair, body, body-shape, skin, skin tones, and skin quality. I began noticing women because they utilized many of the different products marketed to them and had the ability to adorn themselves. During the Sixties, the period in which I was growing up, fashion was particularly fascinating, and as a child I was very aware of my surrounding world. Later I began studying the images in magazines and advertisements religiously; but what caught my attention most was the fashion and beauty happening in my own home.

My mother was a major beauty influence in my early life. She was the first person in whom I noticed a visible and dramatic change in beauty. We did not have a lot of money in my family, particularly when we were young children. But I noticed that when my mother would get dressed to go out with my father after a day of taking care of the kids, she had an allure that seemed so much richer than the quality of life we were actually living. The transformation was extraordinary and I marveled at her. I knew her closets weren't filled with luxury garments from the popular designers, nor did she study the trends in *Vogue;* she never attended fashion week, never walked a runway. And yet my mother, with very few obvious effects, had an unquestionable sense of style. She gave me the ability to know there was more to fashion than just clothes and make-up; she taught me that what one wanted in life was revealed not only in how one appeared to the world, but in one's actions. What you want out of life is how you look and behave in life – a conviction that comes from a place deep inside us.

Years later as I went through school, it wasn't so much that I would envision how people should look outwardly, but that I would get an intuitive feeling of what they were actually trying to say "behind" their appearance. Everyone, I observed, had a story to tell, and through that story they were communicating what they really wanted. For example, if someone projected an image of genuineness, kindness or a desire to inspire others, I knew these values were very important to them. I wanted to help each person appear in the world based on their personal truth, so that what they projected would be clear and in alignment. I believe helping people in this way is part of my purpose in life.

Most of us suspect there is something greater, something more than just what we've been told about beauty all our lives. We want to know what beauty personally means to us. Finding beauty in your own life is a far different experience than someone telling you in a magazine or ad, "This is what beauty looks like," "Wear this and you'll be beautiful." Mind you, we love beauty and fashion magazines; they serve a grand purpose of allowing us to visualize what is happening in the world today. Committing to your beautiful self, however, also requires acceptance and courage, and often means facing your perceived limitations. Sometimes we have to walk through a little "ugly" to get to our beauty.

When I worked in make-up, I remember a young woman I was mentoring whom I'll call Cathy. Cathy had the ability, the art and the skills to be a wonderful make-up artist, but she had an overpowering fear; she was afraid her skills as a make-up person required validation on every level. The fear in her life held her back severely. I knew her fear was not real – meaning it didn't have the power to stop her true potential – but it was real for her and that had to be acknowledged. The fear was so real, in fact, that when she took a step towards her vision, she was often too paralyzed to take any action and left the room in tears. We could not move forward with her career until we explored her relationship with herself and her purpose.

*When you are in your truth,
every step you take and every
choice you make each day
means that you are more
aligned with self.*

It may seem a little strange to open a book on beauty and find the word purpose. When I consult with individual clients, the first set of questions they ask me usually pertains to enhancing their physical beauty – how they should style their hair or make-up, how to change their body, or what to do to look younger. I appreciate these questions, and while they are relevant for many of us, that's not where I believe the conversation about beauty begins. Many of us know, even when we read all the articles, change our hairstyle, change our bodies, or buy the wardrobe, it isn't necessarily a guarantee that we'll end up feeling or being more beautiful. If we are talking about the true transformational power of beauty, we have to go deeper. We have to go to the source of who we really are or know ourselves to be, from within.

This is in no way meant to suggest that physical beauty and proper self-care have no relationship to this process. When we know who we are and radiate from our true inner being, we often feel inspired to take better care of ourselves, to eat well, to wear the colors and the make-up and accessories that make us feel excited to be alive. What I am positing here is that if we only focus on the externals when approaching the conversation of what it means to be beautiful, we miss a fundamental aspect of who we are. We may also miss part of our lives.

You can't do anything in life with true conviction until you recognize your purpose. Your purpose aligns you, takes you directly to your source, and allows you to learn more about you, because this work is only – only – about your relationship with yourself.

A client once asked me in tears, "Why am I so scared to be beautiful?". As I shared with her, beauty requires something of you and you alone. All beauty begins with self-love. It doesn't require anyone else. It is not something that anyone can give you. You can't gather all your family and friends and say, "Let's do this together." You have to be willing to do this for yourself. You can work with others, of course, and use them for inspiration, as they may be inspired by you. You can even work with the ideas in this book in groups. But the decision to be beautiful is one which everyone must come to on their own.

In Truth of Beauty: The Path To Uncovering A Beautiful You, I have created eight steps or principals, each with a chapter devoted to it, that will take you through the Truth of Beauty process: Trust, Discover, Describe, Visualize, Accept, Appear, Own and Commit. Trust is where you begin to lay your foundation, it is your entry point. In order to experience beauty in your life you must trust your personal truth. Discover ignites the process of finding who you are and your purpose – the "two words" which you will use as the cornerstones of creating your beautiful life. Describe continues the refinement process of putting that purpose into action. Visualize is how you see yourself and your purpose enacted in the world; what you want to create. Accept prepares you for the way your relationships will change; your relationship to self, and to others. Appear is what you put out in the world, how your beauty is seen and experienced by you and by others. Own means taking full responsibility for your beauty and your life, claiming your beauty fully as your own. Commit is your final dedication to your purpose and integrates all the other steps. When you are committed to your own beauty you are confident in yourself and fearless of others. With commitment you'll know what it means to dedicate your life to your truth – which is what a life of beauty is.

While a series of "steps" may sound like work to some, the concepts in this book are less about something you need to know and more about principles to follow. Often questioning even one aspect of what we've been taught will open up a dynamic world of new possibilities. I have designed this book with the intention that it should be accessible and easy to reference, something to inspire you daily and remind you at all times of your beautiful self. It is my hope that you will discover in these pages a beauty that is yours to claim, a beauty that endures, that radiates, and, most importantly, that never goes out of style.

Wishing you a beautiful life!

Curtis Quinntin Phelps
New York City

Trust

In order to be fully beautiful, you have to be in truth. And there is no way to get to truth unless you trust yourself.

Trust comes first because it is our foundation, we can't build anything without it. In order to do this work, we need to know that we are safe to explore who we are. We need to trust ourselves. We must reach that place of what we know to be true; not what our mother or father, or grandfather, or best friend, or society told us about ourselves. And the only way to get there is through trust.

I am aware that for some of us trust can be a very loaded word. Usually, when people speak about trust, they use the word in relation to experiences with other people in which they have trusted and been disappointed. "I don't trust him," "You know you really can't trust her", "I'll never trust you again." The word "trust" can bring up feelings of sadness, grief, or even hatred. We may mourn a time when we felt we once trusted and don't feel we can trust anymore. Or when we are asked to trust, we may look at someone suspiciously as if they were trying to sell us something. "What do I have to do? How much is it going to cost me?" This is ironic when you consider the question: what is it costing you in life *not* to trust yourself?

Most everyone from a very early age has a pure direction in life, an intuitive sense of what is near and dear to their being. That direction comes from within – what you want, who you are and who you know yourself to be. One day that self is challenged or questioned at the core, forcing you to question yourself, how you see yourself, how others see you. There is usually some pain involved. In order to avoid more pain, we become conditioned to behave in a certain way, beginning the process of abandoning our true self. The conditions we inherit take over and seem to define us, and we stop trusting ourselves. We may even feel we are "fighting for our lives" – arguing with others, angry and adrift, because it feels as if someone else has the key to our inner door now and they've locked us out.

When this occurs, we conduct our lives from the outside looking in, pounding at the back door to get to what we want, instead of walking through the front door of truth. The subtext of the argument is the soul-cry, "You don't see me, you aren't giving me what I want!" But at this point others often don't know or can't give us what we want. We must look within.

We all want to have an experience of trust. Anger often results from the frustration that we are looking for someone to lead us back to trusting ourselves. When you are truly in trust, you feel acceptance for yourself, for others and for what is. We need to locate that place where trust happens from within, where we don't have to be angry because no one is withholding anything from us. We must know that at the deepest level trust doesn't have anything to do with another person, even though they may reflect our experience of trust back to us. Trust always begins with the self.

Trust assumes that we don't have to invent or go into the world looking for our beauty. It is already there, whether we can see it or not. We all know that there are incidents and situations that can throw us out of a state of trust. You're not in alignment, you're outside yourself. You are acting based on what you have learned or what others have told you; you are relating to your life from a conditioned response. While that may be a familiar habit, and it may occasionally get you what you want, it is important to know that that isn't who you are, and it isn't where your true beauty lies.

When you look to uncover the beauty you bring to the world, you need to be able to know that there is a self to work with, the fundamental "I" in the words "I am". This is deeper than just your image. Trust is knowing that "I" have come to the planet for a specific purpose, that "I" can trust that what comes from the deepest part of my soul is what makes me happy, that my purpose is there for a reason, and that I'm brave enough to honor that purpose.

In my own personal journey with trust, it took me a while to understand the important relationship between trust and beauty. Most of us trust ourselves sometimes, other times we don't. We go through life without much awareness, and experiences just seem to happen to us. We may even feel on top of the world one day or victimized the next, but it's all based on externals; what or who is out there "doing this" to us. We need someone else's permission or approval to take a step, and if something goes wrong, we then blame them or look to the past to what someone told us to do or who they expected us to be. We will never find our beauty that way.

When we are afraid to trust, it is very difficult to share our beauty with the world; everything becomes a negotiation. We are constantly in a state of bargaining our power, dominating, or asking for permission just to "be". Or we are constantly seeking, only pursuing what we are told we should want. This may work for a while, but eventually the rules change, or one group expects us to be one thing and another group something else, and we self-destruct. Or we become bland, generic, and essentially drift through life without a purpose, unsure of who we are or what we want, which is another definition of not trusting the self.

Before we go any further, I'd like to talk about the use of the word "want" in the Truth of Beauty context. We all want things, of course, from the businessperson who wants to sign the new client, to the couple who wants to go to Bali for their honeymoon. There is nothing wrong with wanting. What we are looking for is the "want" that comes from a profound place of knowing within us. It's stronger than a preference, and it is as personal as your signature. This is a want that conjures up a feeling or emotion of personal satisfaction that is solely intended for you. This want is based on who you are and leads to your purpose in the world.

What does that look like? I'll be honest: sometimes, when we are on a search for our truth for the first time, it isn't easy to tell. There is a type of wanting, for example, that is very similar to craving comfort food. Ice cream is delicious, and there are times when we want ice cream and that's fine, but there are also moments when we know the ice cream we are eating is a substitute for something else – comfort or love. What we truly want is deeper than any temporary craving. What we are looking for here is what you really want.

One clue that your want is aligned with truth is that it is unique to you, feels good and is always in your best interest. It fulfills you completely, and you get a "Yes!" feeling in your soul when you honor it. It is the foundation of the Truth of Beauty work that, on the deepest level, you know what you want, it's just that sometimes you can't locate it. Or you don't know how to express it (or feel you have forgotten it). The good news is, it is always there. You will hear me say it many times: your beauty is locked in your purpose, and uncovering your purpose requires trust. That is why committing to yourself is so important to this process.

In the professional world of beauty, we often have clients who sit in our chair in a boutique, store or salon, and who say, in one form or another, the iconic phrase, "Make me beautiful". It's not an outrageous request - as a make-up artist and beauty consultant that's my job. But often the question is much more complex than it sounds. Despite the vision I may have for someone based on what I think he or she wants, for the client who doesn't trust, the results can be disappointing.

A very good example of this is someone I'll call Deborah, with whom I consulted during my time as a make-up artist. She was physically a very beautiful woman, a socialite, someone with money, education, homes, and status in her community. She was also part of an elite circle of wealthy women. Yet when she attended social functions, she felt small amongst the others, as if she hadn't quite "arrived". The instruction, what she said she wanted when she came to me, was to appear "bigger" in life – feminine and statuesque.

Because I was still developing my understanding about trust, I didn't know at that time that Deborah and I needed to begin with a conversation about what "bigger" meant to her, both in terms of her purpose and how she saw herself. Instead, we dove right in. As we began to work together, I immediately knew something was off in our session but I didn't trust that feeling. Anything I did was suspect to her. When I applied make-up she flinched slightly, or stopped my hand outright, questioning every single choice I made. Her face seemed to say, "I can already feel this won't look right for me." And we had only just started!

She was obviously frustrated with the session and I began to feel fear, which is not where you want to be with a client as a trusted professional. I ended up doing something to try to pacify the situation, offering what I thought was best, but she remained unhappy throughout the session. She didn't trust herself, and so she could not trust me.

What I realized later was that Deborah was trying to impress everyone else in order to feel secure. Deborah was unable to see how she was different from the others even if they belonged to the same social group; she wasn't looking for her personal truth, she was trying to be aligned with the group's identity before she was aligned with her own. She was asking to be "bigger," but whenever anything in life encouraged her to really step up, the actual experience of bigness made her uncomfortable, which was part of her conditioning. Afraid and scared to step beyond her comfort zone, I knew that she was longing for a deeper connection with her true self.

Deborah reminded me of another client in a similar position, Sue. Sue always had the right sunglasses, the trendy handbags, the latest style, but at almost six feet she still felt she looked "small", like a little girl in mommy's closet: nothing fitted right or seemed to belong to her. Someone told Sue what was fashionably correct and because she had the money she went out and immediately bought it. But it wasn't integrated in her spirit and it didn't reflect her truth, and so, frustrated, she often just went and bought something new to feel good. I've worked with several men with the same problem.

You don't have to be wealthy or a socialite to understand exactly how Deborah, or Sue, or so many others have felt. From the most expensive boutique to the thrift store, or wherever one shops in between, it is not uncommon for many of us to appear one way to the world but to feel very differently within. The goal is to get to a place of integration where we are whole because we care more about who we are, and are not defined by what we have or can buy.

The experience of not trusting yourself is different, by the way, from occasionally feeling uncertain, which we all experience from time to time. It is all right to walk into a store and genuinely not have a specific style. Asking for a professional opinion, weighing options, seeking advice, are not always signs of lack of trust. I'm talking about something much more powerfully felt, a deeper insecurity, a lack of knowing that leaves us unmoored, like a ship drifting out to sea. Usually I have found that with this feeling comes a sense of panic, a desperation that demands attention: "Who will tell me what I'm supposed to want? Who will define me for me?"

Another client, Elizabeth, came into the salon fully aware of what she wanted. Strong, dominant, the moment she walked in the room it was clear she was in charge. She also arrived in a state of uncertainty – she was open to suggestions. But her expectation was clear: she had a very important meeting with some potential investors in her company and she wanted to appear powerful. I gave her a very relaxed look, not too much foundation, eyes or powder; clean, with a bold red lipstick. It might not have worked on others, but with her simple black ponytail and minimalist fashion choices, it was perfect for her.

What I am focusing on here is that, after working with or observing the work of thousands of people, I am still impressed by the fact that many of us are afraid, or think it is inappropriate, to ask for exactly what we want. We hesitate to bring the kind of trust to our lives that announces when we walk into the room that the guessing games are over. Here is my truth. I trust myself, who I am and what I want. We often call that confidence. It radiates from us as we move through the world. This is also the definition of style.

The examples of trust are everywhere, if we look for them. Hundreds of chances to trust ourselves are presented to us in the course of a week, experiences that reveal us to ourselves, and also opportunities to see how others trust or don't trust themselves. And there is no judgment, as we are all learning. What I have also come to realize through this work is that everything in our life, good or bad, offers us another opportunity to discover our truth, to help us see where we need to learn to trust ourselves. The essence of trust is faith in yourself.

I'd like you to try and recall a time when you were very young and you knew what it was like to trust yourself, a time when you believed that you could do or be anything you wanted. Think: 'I can do that!" Go back as far as you can remember. Later in life you may have suspected that you couldn't do everything, or rather, someone else said you couldn't do something and you listened, and stopped trusting yourself. We always want to get back to the place of trusting ourselves regardless of what has occurred in our lives. Trust creates the sacred relationship we need to have with self in order to find our purpose, and which ultimately leads us to our beauty.

I will often ask my clients, particularly the ones who have the greatest challenge in trusting themselves, to remember a time when they made a decision or achieved a goal based on something they wanted. In other words, they trusted what they wanted and went after it – a want that didn't come from anyone else but them. Some people have to go very far back in their history to find an example of trust, sometimes even back to early grade school. But how long ago it happened isn't important. What matters is for you to remember the feeling of what it meant to trust yourself.

I asked Scott, one of my clients who was struggling with depression, to remember a time when he trusted himself and had a pleasing outcome. The pleasing outcome is also very important, because it is a feeling; and change often begins with our being moved or motivated by an emotional response. It's not required, but it definitely helps. In Scott's case, his experience growing up was one of shame: he had been bullied at school, often teased because of his physical appearance. Before he left for college, Scott completely changed his look, began to work out, and got a lot of new attention with his new body. He acknowledged that while he enjoyed the way he appeared and the attention he often received, there was still something missing in his life, even to this day; a sense of feeling secure within himself.

*Trust is the sacred relationship
we have with self in order to
find our purpose, and which
ultimately leads us to beauty.*

It was after a longer conversation that Scott shared with me the time when he most felt connected to his life. He described his childhood love of drawing, especially around the age of seven. Drawing had been life-affirming to him at that age; he loved the sketch book and pens his grandmother had given him for his birthday, he'd even entered an art contest for kids at the local library and won. He'd trusted his talent by entering the contest and it had led to a pleasing outcome. Scott was able to discover that trust for him once involved creating beautiful work as an artist. He knew what he wanted, he believed in himself. As a result of this realization and reconnecting to this memory, Scott was able to bring a feeling of trusting himself back into his life, creating an emotional re-charge that began to propel him forward in our work together. You will read more of Scott's story later in this book.

I, too, can recall a time from childhood when I trusted myself and had a pleasing outcome, even though it definitely wasn't the outcome I anticipated. I was five years old and had mustered up enough courage to speak with my father about an allowance. Now, I didn't have much of a one-on-one relationship with my father – there were eight of us children. And I was very afraid of my father because I felt, even at that age, that I was a bit "light" in his eyes, I wasn't cut from the same macho cloth as him. I knew, even at five, that he didn't care for the things I already cared for.

I went into the room where he was relaxing after work and said to him, "Dad, I need to speak to you about something."

"What do you need to speak about?"

"I would like an allowance," I told him. I was very serious.

"An allowance?" he replied, somewhat intrigued. "Well, what are you going to do with it?"

"I would like to save up for a toy." I loved putting things together at that age, and there was a model airplane I wanted that I had seen in a local store.

Not only did he not give me the allowance, he then began to lecture me: "Your allowance is the food you eat, the bed you sleep in, the shoes you wear on your feet, the roof over your head, the heat that…." He went through a whole list of things that were my "allowance", while I just stood there listening.

When he finished, I remember feeling my heart sink, and I also remember thinking, "How do I walk out of this room right now without him knowing that I'm hurt by what he said?" And I kept thinking, "Don't cry. Whatever you do don't cry."

Reading this now, you may be surprised by the way the story ends. You might have assumed, as this is a story about a pleasing outcome, that my father gave me the allowance I asked for and I ran to the store that same day and bought the toy I wanted. This is the outcome that would have happened in the movies.

But the point of the story, as I see it, is that it was a very big deal for me to walk in and ask my father for that allowance. I knew intuitively that we didn't have a lot of money in those years and that he probably would say no. But something in me said, "If he says no, it's okay. You have to go in and ask because this is something you really want." And I trusted myself to go to him, regardless of the outcome.

That experience with my father was a major moment of trust in my life. Although the outcome might not seem very pleasing to many of you reading this, it was right for me. I had never had that kind of nerve before as a kid. Though in my heart of hearts I'd suspected I was strong, I'd already developed early "conditioning" by that age that I was using to get by. People had labeled me a crybaby. The "crybaby" had the experience of getting attention, which I got, but through the shadow. In other words, I learned I could cry to get what I needed. It sometimes worked, but I already knew at five that this wasn't what I wanted for my life. I don't mean to suggest in any way here that boys shouldn't cry. I could have gone to my room and cried. But if I had cried with the sole intention of manipulating my father into feeling sorry for me, that would not have been my truthful self or powerful. My outcome was pleasing, not because of the money, but because I saw myself after that day as stronger than I'd ever been. I'd trusted what I wanted regardless of the outcome, and I'd asked for it. I knew from that day forward I could trust myself.

I have returned to this story many times in my own "beauty recovery". Even though I have other memories more recent, it takes me to an emotional place and reminds me what trusting myself feels like. It's a great feeling! Sometimes in order to find our trust again, we have to move through unpleasantness as we uncover the truth of who we really are. It's part of our commitment to ourselves.

Uncovering your beauty requires effort. It requires time, energy, action and, most importantly, a tireless and dedicated commitment to self. It is not that beauty has to be scary, but sometimes we resist being truthful with ourselves because we're afraid of more pain. And because of our conditioned and learned habits, we may decide it's too much work, and give up. What is required is for you to be present, for you to recognize your thoughts and take responsibility for them. Some people would rather stay in the familiar because they know that experience inside and out. When we are defensive and upset because we don't trust ourselves, we feel powerless and blame everyone.

We may be tempted or conditioned to use our history as our calling card, not because we are bad people but because it is what we know as familiar. We fight to be seen, fight to be acknowledged. It becomes a painful experience, going into the world trying constantly to "get" what we need externally, what I call the "great beauty rip-off." We are trying to attain something spiritual from the outside, thinking that it will ultimately transform us, or we run around asking everyone what they think of us – beauty by consensus – instead of recognizing that we already are what we are looking for. When you are in your beauty, there is no "getting" from anyone else, no need for approval and no fight. When you're fighting, you're not trusting. We need to remember that truth has its own resilience; even if we are in circumstances that are unfavorable, we can always commit to a beautiful life when we are in our truth. Your beauty isn't based on circumstance, but truth.

Once you connect to a feeling of trust, no matter how far back you have to go, you will return to a place of alignment. I can't emphasize enough how essential this is. What's important here is that all of us, at some point in our lives, trusted ourselves, and that that is the power we need to rely on. The essence of trust is faith in self. Faith in self will lead you to the ultimate question: "Where is my beauty? What is it and what does it look like?"

Trust begins with believing in yourself. All the work proceeds from there. You have to trust yourself just to be okay with learning about yourself. It takes great trust in yourself to say, "I'm going to go 'in' and study me" and "I'd like to have a better relationship with myself." Trust restores us to a place from which we can move forward. We may not have all the answers when we begin, but in trust we are determined to find them.

So, stop the fight and just be. Yes, it requires some work, but it is worth it. And how does it look and feel when you get there? Sensational. Remember, you are already putting your energy into the world, you can't not give the world your energy. You might as well put out that energy with a clear intention and be clear about what you want.

This is the moment that matters. We need your beauty now. You have come to the planet because you have a purpose, and if you don't allow the world to experience that purpose, then you hold back on the world and even more you hold back on yourself. Sickness begins when we withhold from ourselves the things that we love and what we are. And that's tragic, because love of self is where the greatest love begins. You are worth your own trust. How we build on that trust to uncover our beauty through purpose is the next stage.

Discover

True beauty occurs the moment you discover: your truth is who you are.

Discovering your truth leads to living openly as your beautiful self, who you intuitively know yourself to be. A theme in the work of the mystic Joseph Campbell encourages us: "Follow Your Bliss." The spiritual teacher Esther Hicks inspires us to discover through trusting our deepest emotions what makes us most joyful and to commit to that in our lives. Philosopher Jiddu Krishnamurti once said, "You must know for yourself, directly, the truth of yourself, and you cannot realize it through another, however great. There is no authority that can reveal it. Truth can be uncovered only through self-knowledge." And inscribed above the entrance to the ancient temple of Apollo at Delphi were the words: "Know yourself."

There are many wonderful teachers who have carried this message to the world for centuries. Their words may be different, but the conclusion is the same:

the foundation of a beautiful life and what makes you beautiful is your personal truth; to know who you are, and what you have come to contribute to the world.

In the first step of the process of uncovering, or "discovering" your beauty, we had to begin with the experience of trust. Trust was an essential step in helping build or renew our relationship with self. The decision to trust leads us directly to discovery. Because I trust myself, I can now discover myself. In discovery, we begin to appreciate who we are, and the difference that we will make in life – for ourselves and for society.

When I first began my work of helping others discover their beauty I would begin with the questions, "What does beauty mean to you? What would make you feel beautiful or happy?" I assumed these questions would be received with excitement and enthusiasm and was surprised to discover that some clients were overwhelmed, confused, and even frustrated when I asked them to define what beauty or happiness meant to them.

One woman I worked with, Deena, came to me on the advice of a friend because she was unhappy in her career, and felt that she needed "a new direction" to be fulfilled. She'd changed jobs several years before and even moved across the country for a new position. Although she enjoyed working for the new company, on a fundamental level Deena knew: despite major changes in her circumstances, her life had remained pretty much the same.

It was obvious from the look on her face that these questions in our initial conversation brought up pain. When I asked Deena what was happening for her in that moment, she said through tears that the question, "What makes you happy?" frightened and depressed her. At almost forty years old, she wasn't sure what she wanted in life. She was successful by most people's standards, but unfulfilled. "Most people don't get what they want anyway," she had always been told growing up. She explained, "It's better not to want too much happiness than to be disappointed. I was always taught that security in life meant having an education, a good job, and money in the bank."

I was moved by her honesty and related to it personally. I'd had times in my own life when the idea of following my bliss, while at times very exciting, also felt overwhelming, even painful. As I worked with Deena, she began to trust me and, most importantly, herself. I found it was easier to talk to clients about who they were if I broke the concept down into what I began to call their "two words". The concept of discovering the "two words", which I will refer to throughout this chapter and the rest of the book, is a kind of vital shorthand, if you will, for getting down to the business of understanding one's whole self. In other words, being told to go into the world and find what makes one happy or beautiful may be daunting, but it is hard to be scared of two little words!

Purpose was a scary concept for Deena, but I knew finding her two words would inspire her and would change everything. When she asked again, "How do I fix my life?" I reassured her that when she discovered her two words and committed fully to them, the question of fixing her life would no longer haunt her. Her life did not need "fixing"; by committing to her truth, her life would "fix" itself.

DISCOVERING YOUR FIRST OR "FOUNDATIONAL" WORD

To initiate the two-word process – beginning with your first word and eventually moving on to your second – we must rely on trust as our foundation. In order to find the truth in our two words, and not just come up with something based on our conditioning, we have to trust ourselves to be honest about what we are really feeling. In preparation for helping you discover your own first word, I'd like to share a little more about my session with Deena.

When we began, I wanted Deena to know there was no pressure on her of any kind to prove herself, and I encouraged her to feel as relaxed and comfortable as possible. When she felt safe and open to her own guidance, we began with her first word or foundational word. This word, I explained, would arrive when she considered a simple question: what word comes to you naturally - a word that you can trace back to youth - that has been with you most of your life, that continues to show up in your world with powerful meaning, a word that seems to pursue you, that you can't get rid of? You may not like it, you may love it, you may keep it a secret, you may go into the world shouting it from the rooftops, but it is a word that speaks to your heart, the most significant word of your life. This word offers you a sense of direction, like a guide, asking you to follow it. It comes to you with a meaning only you understand and believe in. When you consider this word, you may feel extremely vulnerable, perhaps emotional. This is a word that touches the depths of your soul.

At first, Deena admitted that sadness had been something she felt at many points in her life, and that she often felt angry. While it was important for her to acknowledge these feelings, I explained that sadness and anger were responses to her conditioning, not the meaning or intent behind her first word. She would know her first word because, even though sadness and anger might come up for her during the process, her first word would give her a feeling of relief and a deep sense of knowing, feelings that she had when she once trusted herself. I encouraged her to return to our conversation about trust if she needed to, in order to ground herself in finding her first word.

*Discovering your truth
leads to living openly as
your beautiful self, who you
intuitively know yourself
to be.*

I then sat silently as Deena considered her word. As much as I wanted to help based on what I already sensed about her, I resisted. It is hard to tell anyone what their first word should be, no matter how well you think you know them; any way of directing them to what their word is can be a means of controlling the outcome. I wanted Deena to have the same experience I had with my first word.

I found my first word when I posed a question to myself: what is it in my life that seems important to me, that, no matter which way I turn, is always there? I had been going through a challenging time understanding myself, and I needed to know my truth: what was most essential to my being? Or what existed in my life which, if I got rid of everything else, was the one thing that remained? It probably won't surprise many of you reading this: my foundational word was "Beauty".

And yet, my word was still somewhat shocking to me. I committed myself to beauty, lived and breathed it, but still had moments of shame, especially when someone said I should consider a career in teaching or finance, rather than one deciding what color eyeshadow would go perfectly with a silver gown. Even then, I knew intuitively that beauty was about more than make-up, but I wasn't in a place to understand the depths of why it was important to me. I was a perfect example of what it means to battle with self. I went to beauty school, became a makeup artist and fashion consultant. Everything I did was related to beauty, though I couldn't admit it to myself; but when I looked at my life the evidence was there. I left my hometown, a place that had its own beauty, because I needed to find a place where beauty was an industry and where it was a constant conversation - one that people took seriously.

Beauty was a word that was always there in my life, but as much as I was devoted to beauty, I was also embarrassed by it. I was taught early in life that to be interested in beauty was to be vain, weak, and frivolous. And in some people's estimation, to be interested in beauty meant that I was "effeminate" or "not a man". So, if someone had asked me my word at that time, I probably would have come up with several other words, words that I felt were more "important" and that would have pleased the people I knew – family, friends, teachers. Anyone but me, who knew my truth.

My point here is that my whole life was spent devoted to the importance of beauty, and yet on the outside I was still defending myself and what I loved against society and the world, worried that people would see me as shallow and superficial. I was fighting against who I was and what was innate in me, and yet I often wondered why I was so frustrated at times and why, on the occasions when I felt I looked beautiful, true beauty seemed to elude me from within. My whole relationship to my life changed when I finally began to trust myself and embrace my word. My own process of discovery began that day, a process that has carried me, and that I hope will carry you, to realizing your beauty.

After a brief exercise to get Deena to a place of trust within herself, she responded almost immediately. Her first word, she told me, was "Power". Her entire life, as she envisioned it, had been defined by power. While the idea of being powerful made her happy, life had often been a power struggle, and the struggle continued. I asked her to explain. She related, tearfully, that she had grown up the oldest girl in a traditional family where she was expected to take care of her brothers and younger sisters. Deena was considered "out of control" at an early age because she often questioned the rules. She didn't want to take care of anyone or play with the "girly" toys that were given her; she enjoyed sports. She complained as a child that the freedoms her brothers enjoyed and the way she restricted as a girl were unfair. She'd gone through a very difficult rebellious stage as an adolescent.

There was even an incident when she'd been accused of stealing something from a mall; the girls who were actually guilty all pointed the finger at her. Her parents were mortified and begged her to admit she was guilty – the manager said he wouldn't call the police if she returned the merchandize and apologized. She was adamant; despite being shouted at by a security guard and humiliated by the adults around her for what felt like hours, she refused to back down. Eventually, she was banned from the store but allowed to go home. She explained that despite the fact that the experience was horrifying, she had a sense of herself and her power that she'd never had before. "I would have gone to jail or a group home that night, and my mother and father knew it, before I lied that I'd done something wrong."

Deena had had a series of experiences as a young woman that had been disappointing; partners who felt that she was "headstrong" and independent, professors in college who didn't appreciate having their ideas challenged; and there were many times when she felt uncomfortable and different, not sure exactly how to get along with men or with some women. The general consensus among her friends and family was that while Deena was inspiring in her accomplishments, she was "too much" and would probably end up successful, but alone.

But along with the personal frustrations she'd had growing up, there were also triumphs. She'd been an activist in college and got some gender-biased policies changed because of her determination. She'd distinguished herself at several corporations where she'd been an executive, and despite the male-dominated atmosphere, she was known as fearless and outspoken. She'd been part of the leadership team of an organization and won an award the year before that recognized "powerful women."

A friend told her that she had a reputation at work for being cut-throat, ruthless and tough, and while these were suggested to be positive attributes, Deena went into a depression soon after. It felt like a repetition of her childhood, of being "too much". People were so focused on her power they couldn't see her underlying tenderness. She'd feared that maybe they couldn't see her tenderness because perhaps it didn't exist anymore.

I acknowledged, from my own experience of being bullied about beauty, that the world doesn't always embrace our first word. There were times when my relationship with my first word was deeply fulfilling personally, as I've shared earlier, but also extremely painful. But the main criterion we use to determine our first word isn't about how our word is received by others, it's the fact that this word has been a significant, defining presence in all our experiences. Getting to a point where we are able to experience the full power of our first word, no longer with pain and fear but with confidence and radiance, is what this process is about.

Being honest about her first word meant that when we discussed power, Deena had to acknowledge the shadow side of being seen as powerful. Some admired her strength, but others saw her as hard, angry, or aggressive. And what caused her great anxiety was that secretly she feared she was becoming all of those things. She felt shut down emotionally. Now she was at a point in her career and personal life where being "powerful" made her feel exhausted. She felt impatient, brittle, and easily exasperated. During a recent first date, she walked out halfway because her date said something that "pissed her off." She felt ready to snap at a moment's notice. There had been scenes recently in stores. She still felt powerful, but power had become an ugly word that meant feeling isolated and alone. She still won her battles, as always, but who wanted to be at war all the time?

DISCOVERING THE SECOND OR "ASPIRATIONAL" WORD

When Deena returned to the process and felt that she was committed to her first word, it was time to explore her second.

The second, or aspirational word, is related to the first, but the second word plays a very different and essential role in discovering one's truth. This word describes a quality that we sometimes feel we are lacking; a quality which, if we had more of it, would enable us to manifest our first word fully in the world. Often our second or "aspirational" word is a trait that we aspire to or admire in others and wish we had in greater supply. In defining your second word, you may recall saying to yourself at some point in the past, "If only I had more of this aspect in my life, then I would really be able to be myself." The second word is not meant to shame or belittle us; it is an exploration into what we need to make ourselves whole, or where we feel our power exists outside ourselves. In other words, what we believe we require in order to express our first word with confidence. We will explore later the unique role this pivotal word plays, eventually leading us to our greatest inspiration.

My second or aspirational word is – Strength. I chose Strength because when I fully acknowledged to myself that my first word was Beauty, I knew that I would need to be strong to challenge the resistance I felt inside and from the others around me. I was fighting to be strong because I believed I had been conditioned to think of myself as weak. Strength from within would be required for me to bring beauty fully into the world.

The method I recommend for finding your two words is really very simple: go to a quiet place, sit down, relax, and find the trusting place within. Do not be surprised if your two words come to you in seconds or if nothing comes to mind at first. Some of my clients have early conditioning that is very strong, so sticking with the process until you hear your words is vital. Do not judge yourself or worry about "doing it wrong." The most important thing is to remain open-minded, and to listen.

After asking yourself the questions that lead to the discovery of your first word, please write this foundational word down before moving onto the second word. Your two words are not a "goal" you must achieve. They are a part of you, as familiar as a receiving a call from an old friend. You may not have heard from her or him in a while, but you know the loving connection remains. Remember: the best way to find your words is to concentrate on what life continues to point out to you as a direction. Some people are suspicious because it seems so basic, so clear; they need it to be more complicated, but it's not. Remember, your first word suggests a direction in life that you have always known, your second word is the quality you feel you need to bring your first word into the world. As you begin the journey of finding your own two words, know that there are endless possibilities and combinations to choose from. You'll know you've arrived when you get there.

I asked Deena for a quality she felt she needed in order to bring the experience of her first word to fruition. Without her second word, she might have a sense of what her truth was but would find it difficult to follow through. This second word would allow her to experience "Power", her first word, in its fullest expression.

I then asked her to relax and imagine that she was going on a journey, to a place she had been before, where calm, comfort and beauty awaited her. I emphasized again the importance of her being vulnerable throughout the entire process, but particularly at this point, because we were now facing some of her greatest fears. She closed her eyes, but I could see by the way she gripped the chair that she was frightened to let go. Her experience of power had led to a lifetime of defensiveness and maneuvers to avoid getting hurt. She apologized for her tears, but I reassured her that it was okay to feel emotion; in fact, it was encouraged. I wanted her to be open and unprotected, and experience again what it feels like to be in total acceptance and self-love. It is only from this place, where we let our guard down and no longer feel judged, that we can truly hear and receive our deepest guidance.

As part of the exercise of discovering her second word, I invited Deena to consider a "tool" she would need for her heroic journey – as someone would take a tent into the mountains or hiking gear. This tool would be with her always, to support her foundational word. It would also give her a feeling of wholeness and help her know, despite any resistance or obstacles she might face, she could trust she'd be fine.

When she came out of the meditation, I asked what her second word was, and she told me, without hesitation, "vulnerability". I asked if any images had come to mind during the meditation. She had a vision of walking along a beach in a flowing dress, almost like a nightgown, a flower in her hair, and barefoot. The sand felt good under her feet and the sun was warm on her shoulders, and she felt at peace. Sometimes she just bent down and scooped up the water, or she sat and threw sand into the sea. The ocean came and washed her bare feet as she sat and watched the sun go down.

As she described the image, I could tell she was embarrassed by what she'd seen. "I feel like I'm describing a TV commercial or something", she said, laughing. She feared the image was too "girly" or feminine and remembered a story that she'd almost forgotten from childhood: an aunt had taken her and her sister shopping for clothes and stopped at the boys' department first because she said if "Deena wants to be a boy, she might as well dress like one." The aunt thought the joke was funny, but Deena was mortified and had cried when they got home, vowing never to trust her aunt again.

I told her that what I observed in her vision wasn't someone who was overly girly or too feminine, but someone who allowed herself the experience of being vulnerable. We sat for a moment in the room in silence and let the words settle in. Moving through her embarrassment about her beach scene, she admitted that she adored the beach, she felt safe there. I asked her when she went home for the next week, to visit her mental beach whenever she felt embattled in her daily life, or when she needed a break. I made it clear that it was important that she embrace all of it, even down to the flower in her hair. I felt her relax for what seemed like the first time since we'd been working together.

For Deena, power and vulnerability had been polar opposites. She often felt that she was forced in life to choose one over the other, or one at the expense of the other. Vulnerability for her had been the same as being a victim; there had been times in her life when she'd suffered rather than ask anyone for help. I could see that she was beginning to see vulnerability as a key tool to realizing what it meant to be truly powerful. While we still had more work to do, I watched her remembering her truth through her two words, Power and Vulnerability, over the next couple of weeks, and the realization made her luminous.

In several of our early sessions together, Deena would return to asking me about her career path. I understood the temptation; it is sometimes hard to shake the idea that if we just change jobs, or locations, or relationships, everything in our life will change. And often it does, for a while. But because we are in a dishonest relationship with our truth, ruled by our conditioning, we end up in the new job or relationship, still dislocated, still insecure about who we are and where we are. I explained that before we could talk about a job, we needed to find out who she was. Part of the transformation for Deena, a self-acknowledged "do-er", was to pause for a moment and relate to her aspirational word and its possibilities. The second word, working in concert with the first word, would guide us down that path.

Working with Deena was a turning-point for me. I began to ask all my clients about their two words. My work as a beauty consultant still involved all the familiar components – make-up, styling, fashion and beauty seminars. But I found that in my beauty conversations, there was also a deeper psychological or spiritual component. Helping someone realize their fullest potential meant asking them about their two words; no beauty conversation is complete now without it.

Most of my clients feel this exercise is part of a fun game and are willing to "play", unaware of how powerful the two words are in their lives and what impact they have on being and living beautifully. It continues to be my deepest conviction that every one of us knows his or her truth and that each of us has two words that help reveal who we are.

Among the clients I have worked with, I am fascinated by people who are harder to read, whose two words don't come as easily as they have to other clients. Some people seem to need more encouragement to dig deeper, while others seem to walk into a room almost as if their two words preceded them.

One woman I met, whom I'll call Ashley, really had me stumped. By the time I met Ashley, I was beginning to pride myself on the fact that I could coach most people into arriving at their words fairly quickly. I wanted to attribute this to great skill on my part, but the fact is, when one trusts oneself, the two words are usually right there, and don't require weeks of unearthing. In most cases, when someone's two words don't come to the surface right away, it has less to do with aimless "searching", and more with the fear of humiliation or of being made to feel wrong.

Ashley and I met briefly more than once at social gatherings (I was the close friend of a woman she worked with). On this occasion, I saw her standing by a window in a crowded room, in what seemed like a private reverie, and I approached her. We had spoken generally about my beauty consulting before. I found Ashley very beautiful and fascinating, possessing her own unique style, and I was curious to know more about her. I explained to her the work I was doing, and she was enthusiastic. We got drinks and sat down on a sofa. An hour and a half later, we were still sitting there, getting nowhere. I felt like the archetypal defeated shoe salesman in front of the exasperated customer, surrounded by a sea of boxes and tissue paper. Nothing we came up with "fitted" Ashley. I realized with dread that the party was coming to an end, and I was about to leave her that evening without even her first word. This was personally appalling for me!

The process had worked so well for others. My confidence in my ability, which had led to results with so many others, was now on the verge of being shattered. Most of all, I felt as if I had abandoned Ashley, because I had promised her that we'd find her words. I registered the slight look of disappointment on her face as we said goodbye. "I know, I'm a bit complicated," she acknowledged. "It was nice seeing you again, Quinntin. Thank you for trying."

I thought about Ashley for days and realized later why I had failed her: Ashley had told me her words, told me twice in fact, but I found it hard to believe them because of what I had observed in her. The words we had returned to, after several tries, were "Friendship" and "Outspoken". In our conversation that day, I made the mistake of not being convinced by her first word, which meant I hadn't been able to move on to her second. I registered the words she gave me but had dismissed them and encouraged her to go a little deeper.

I'll be the first to admit it: it's a little tricky sometimes finding one's two words. In most cases, what comes up right away is usually inspired by genuine insight, but sometimes one's immediate response is what one has been conditioned to want by others, what a friend of mine, Matt, calls "the press release." When we worked together, he admitted the only two words his parents ever wanted to hear from him were "Law School".

Because Ashley seemed so careful and somewhat withdrawn in every social situation in which I'd met her, I feared that "Friendship" was what she felt she should be saying to me to appear more outgoing, rather than what was the truth about her. In her case, "Friendship" felt more like something designed for a Hallmark card rather than the true, foundational word of the person actually sitting across from me.

A few days later, I was on the phone with the friend I had in common with Ashley, and without betraying any confidence I asked a few questions about her. What I was told gave me a new appreciation for the two words she'd chosen, and an even deeper understanding of how profound the two words can be in one's life. I also gained a new respect for the power of trust: Ashley knew herself, and she had been right about herself all along. I had to acknowledge that I had partly seen Ashley through my own lack of trust.

The Ashley my friend described to me was someone who wasn't about "warm fuzzies", perfect gifts on birthdays, or someone who randomly calls to chat or says, "Drop everything and let's meet for coffee!" Ashley, it seemed, was actually very private and had no frivolous side. If anything, she was a bit awkward on the phone unless it was business. But, my friend continued, she'd known Ashley for years and, "if ever you're in a situation where you need someone at 3 a.m. Ashley is the first call you make." She was confident in this because she'd seen Ashley show up for others: she would be there, keys in hand, purse slung over her shoulder, hair tied back, standing on the side of the road near the broken-down car, or the water leaking from the busted pipes, or in the emergency waiting room. A friend of theirs had been diagnosed with cancer, and when it progressed fairly quickly, Ashley organized the friend's bills, dealt with her medical insurers, and helped with the running of her house.

My friend acknowledged again, Ashley probably wasn't the person with whom you'd plan your next vacation to Cancún, but she was there for that sick friend of theirs every day while the woman was in the hospital, even feeding her kids and taking them to school. It didn't matter what was going on in her personal life. You could count on her, my friend told me, she was the archetype of a great friend.

And "Outspoken", the quality she'd chosen for her second word, was what Ashley felt she required to get over an almost debilitating shyness and fear of speaking she'd carried from childhood. She admired outspoken women and felt it was a quality that was necessary in order to be the kind of friend she most envisioned. Being more outspoken, for example, had made it possible for her to confront the hospital staff about her friend's care, and support another friend through a very nasty divorce from an abusive husband. But it hadn't come easy, she'd had to step outside her comfort zone to show up for those experiences. Her second or aspirational word gave her insight into how she hoped to manifest her first word in her life. By committing to speaking out more, Ashley knew she would be able to support her friends in many situations in which her first instinct was to stay home where she could be quiet and safe. She also had dreams of being a child advocate one day and knew that being outspoken was essential to her vision.

I called Ashley days later and resumed our conversation. She was genuinely pleased to hear from me. I acknowledged that "Friendship" and "Outspoken" *were* her words and recognized that she had gone through the process as I'd coached her and offered what had come to her from her place of vulnerability. It was a revelation to me that one could be private, even isolated from people most of the time, and still be a great friend. I began to appreciate that finding one's two words meant going deeper than what appeared on the surface, to ourselves or to anyone else.

If there is one theme I've discovered through my years of work in beauty, it's this: beauty is often not what you think it is or what you've been taught – it's much, much more. If I am in my beauty, I must recognize and acknowledge what beauty is; not what the world tells me, but what it means specifically to me. Far too many of us are not living openly, in our personal truth. We tend to live subconsciously, hiding most of who we are and our true feelings below the surface. This Truth of Beauty step is called discovery because we are bringing who you really are to consciousness, allowing you to know yourself and finally asking: What will I contribute to the world by being completely open, who am I when there is nothing I have to be ashamed of, or feel the need to hide of myself from others?

The world may try to bring us back into the unwanted patterns we know all too well, but with the strength of our two words we will always remember who we are. We sometimes feel that we must rebel to get the world to acknowledge us, which often keeps us mired in the limitations. We're not rebelling against the world in that moment, but against ourselves. Remember: you are only responsible for you. The way to give your beauty to the world is to be at the height of who you truly are. Lovingly resist giving energy to blaming or defensiveness. That which is truly yours needs no defending.

Allow the process of discovery to lead you directly into the next stage, Describe, the step where we refine your truth and begin to define your purpose. Through a greater awareness of self, which is the experience of true beauty, you will become vulnerable enough to feel intuitively what matters most to you. You are your miracle. Love yourself enough to insist on your beautiful life.

Describe

Your purpose is your beauty.

Pause for a moment and consider your reaction to that statement. As I mentioned in the introduction to this book, most of the people I've worked with over the years are surprised to have a conversation about beauty that focuses on one's purpose. In a book on beauty, they expect to find chapters on weight loss or gain, make-up, hair, accessories, exercise, even cosmetic surgery. And yet the discovery of purpose leads us to the most powerful beauty conversation that we may have.

The appreciation of purpose and how it relates to beauty will become clearer as you read this chapter. The most important thing you can bring to this stage of our work is an open mind and a willingness to lose the need to protect yourself. Sensitivity is your guide through this illuminating step. Almost everyone I work with has learned to de-sensitize themselves in order to cope with life, or brace themselves for fear of being hurt or disappointed. But it is exactly that sensitivity which you need to help you identify what your purpose is, to hear your truth speaking to you, loud and clear. Interestingly, it is often the clients in the most obvious pain who are able to surrender the most to the Truth of Beauty process. They have no protection anymore, which means they have no choice but to listen to their own guidance in order to move forward. I am encouraging you at this time to trust yourself as well.

You will hear the word "action" many times throughout Describe because it is vital to understanding what I will call your "third" word – the word that is your purpose in the world. In Describe, you will return to your first or foundational word because it is the description of your foundational word that leads to your purpose. Describe calls on us to deepen our relationship with our first word, to really go in and understand what that word means for us and to locate its special relationship to our lives. Through the process of describing your first word, you will have a greater understanding of how you see your truth in the world – not in a general sense, but in a meaning that is specific for you.

After the discovery of our first and second words (which we will return to later) the step of Describe, and its revelation of purpose in our third word, is a powerful gateway to personal transformation, a major turning-point in committing to your beautiful life.

DESCRIBING THE THIRD (OR "PURPOSE") WORD

On the advice of a friend, Scott came for a Truth of Beauty session at one of the most difficult points in his career. Yet by his appearance one would never have known. Scott arrived for our session in dark jeans and a leather jacket, holding a coffee, with tanned skin and perfectly coiffed hair. He shook my hand firmly, offering a confident smile and a greeting that seemed friendly, but somewhat rehearsed. I immediately observed anger in his blue eyes, but I assumed that with his rugged handsomeness and general affability, most people would find it hard to believe, much less be able to confront Scott on, the evident despair in his life.

For years Scott had been trying to sell his work as an artist, but every time he got closer to achieving success, he managed to sabotage the opportunity. Even more painful than the results of his self-destructive behavior was the fact that he had no idea why he behaved in this way. He hated his job, he'd been through several frustrating romantic relationships, and even though he had family and friends who believed in him and loved him, he often felt like "giving up". He assured me that he wasn't suicidal. Giving up, he explained, meant no longer painting, resigning himself to a job that wasn't inspiring, and finding a partner, not for love, but for convenience – someone to "share the bills". But even that seemed unattainable at times; he didn't hesitate to express his cynicism about the dating process.

As our conversation continued, Scott acknowledged that he could never give up on his art completely, or marry without love, but he felt desperate and didn't know what to do to move forward. When I asked about his other relationships, he admitted that anyone who knew him would say he seemed happy most of the time. Scott's friends experienced him as supportive and kind and knew that he would do anything for the people he loved. He just had a hard time loving himself.

Scott and I had to begin with trust before we could discover his first word. This wasn't easy because of the amount of self-betrayal that had taken place in most of his adult life and most of his childhood – he didn't trust himself anymore. As I described earlier in the chapter on Trust, Scott went back to the time when he was seven and had been bullied at school about his weight. He then told me about the art contest he won with the pencils gifted from his grandmother. It seemed a little silly to him now, but he admitted it was the first time he felt someone recognized his talent, actually saw him for who he was. His mother put his picture on the refrigerator and the family went for ice cream that day. A few years later, Scott told his uncle, "I want to be an artist when I grow up." His uncle told him that artists usually starved and that he'd eventually have to get a real job to support his family.

"My uncle tried to discourage me but I didn't care what he said," Scott said. "I knew deep down that art would be my life. Drawing was one of the only things that made me happy."

I told Scott that if he couldn't trust himself right now, he needed to trust the determined child who wouldn't be dissuaded from following his dream. I asked him to recall the feeling of deep self-knowledge, of feeling right about himself regardless of others' opinions about him. Scott expressed admiration for that boy and acknowledged that this was a time in his life when he felt confident and clear. When we moved on to begin the process of finding his first word, Scott took almost no time at all and said, "I think I know my word already. It's Transformation."

I didn't hide my surprise. "Transformation?"

"In everything I've created, I've wanted to transform people. Even when I was little, I would do things to get my mother's attention to make her happy or get her to laugh. It was the same when I drew pictures and painted through high school. I wanted to shock people or move them in a way that they wouldn't be the same after seeing my work. It's the way I feel when I look at the work of artists I admire."

"Go on."

"I know I could have a job right now doing commercial art and getting paid for it, but I don't want to do magazine ads for selling orange juice, I want to create something that gets noticed, something deeply emotional. When someone hangs my work in their home or in a museum, I need to know it gives them a feeling of love or anger or some emotion, that, whatever it is, people won't just be able to walk past it like pretty wallpaper. They are going to be changed by it!"

I could feel Scott's enthusiasm grow as we continued to discuss what transformation meant to him. In our next session, we moved to uncovering his second, or aspirational, word. After a few minutes of thought, Scott said: "My aspirational word is Audacity. I almost said fearlessness, but audacity is different for me, somehow. If I were to choose the word that would support me in my life in relation to my first word, audacity would be it. I always feel the need to be more audacious in life."

"In what way?" I asked.

"Fearlessness, having courage, standing up to things. Audacity means boldness in my mind, right out front. Perfect for the kind of artist I've always wanted to be. Growing up, I often colored in the lines when I was afraid to get in trouble or get a bad grade. I didn't want kids to laugh at me. But the artists that I admire just say to hell with it, they follow their vision and don't care. I need more audacity in my life. Definitely."

Now aware of his two words and feeling confident about them, Scott was ready to move onto the next step: describing his third word, the word that would lead him to his ultimate purpose.

Sometimes clients ask at this point, "What is the difference between the second and third word? Why did I need to find my second word and how does it relate to my third?" Our second word, you may remember, was a quality we felt we needed in order to bring our first word into being. In order to bring our first word in the world, we needed the empowerment that came from our second word. Now, with that encouragement and insight, we feel we can act. We take our first word, empowered by our second, and go into the world with inspiration. Our third word reveals us to us what we see ourselves doing when we practice our first word. Before we moved on, I shared with Scott a little of my own story. My hope was that it would make the next step of Describe a little clearer for him.

I gave him my two words: Beauty and Strength. Beauty was what most deeply inspired me and Strength was what I often felt I needed more of in life. When I began my initial work of finding my third word, I found it helpful to return to my first word for more in-depth understanding. I was aware that for most people, beauty related only to how someone appeared physically. Or the word might be used to describe the weather – "It's beautiful outside". But whatever others understood beauty to be, or whatever definitions I had been told growing up, I needed beauty to be focused. I had to find out what beauty meant specifically to me.

I was determined to find the one descriptive word that clarified my foundational word, Beauty. Whatever that word was, it would make Beauty personal, it would tell me what action to take to create beauty as I defined it. And that action would lead me to my purpose. It wasn't enough just to explain the word beauty – I needed to go out, to "do" beauty in my everyday life. But I still wasn't sure what that looked like, for me.

After some searching, I came to realize that beauty to me meant Care. Seeing someone simply caring for themselves as well as caring for others had always been deeply inspiring to me. Sometimes this meant a state of being that I called "well-appointed". This brought me back to the memory of my mother and the care she took to be beautiful. Even with modest means, as I mentioned earlier, she cared about beauty, she cared about herself, and therefore those around her. When I saw women and men in life who I knew had taken the time to put together a striking ensemble, even from a very young age I felt excited. I knew that by caring for themselves, by beautifying themselves, they were actively creating a beautiful world.

But caring wasn't just about physical appearance. Caring also meant loving care, being interested in someone else, engaged. With this clarity came a deeper understanding of the role that beauty would play in my own life. It didn't mean that others were wrong if beauty for them exclusively meant fashion, or glamour, or a more aesthetic approach in their lives. That was fine and worked for them. But I knew that for me beauty had to include some form of care or the experience of beauty wasn't complete. The action of beauty in my life would always involve caring. It is often assumed that caring is defined by our relationship with others and what we do for other people. But true caring always starts from within and is as much about one's relationship with self. My third word, my purpose, was Care. And if caring was my purpose, nothing and no one could be excluded from my ability to care.

Scott and I began to explore what his first word, Transformation, meant to him. I asked him how the experience of transformation appeared in his life. I also asked him to take his time as he considered this, and explained that the process of finding his third word, like finding his first and second, was a deeply intimate one. We weren't filling out a questionnaire or a quiz at the back of a magazine while sitting in a doctor's office. I needed him to go inside, to trust his heart, and even if it was sometimes painful, to listen to exactly what he heard.

I then asked him to describe what he saw himself doing when he thought of transformation. The emphasis here was on action; when he considered transformation, what action was taking place for him in that moment?

A few ideas came to mind at first, he said: transformation meant inspiring others, encouraging them. It could also mean confrontation or challenge; coaching others to be powerful and changing their lives in a positive way.

I reminded Scott again that we weren't looking for the definition of the word. A definition will never lead us to our beauty, but action will. I told him to take all the time he needed, but the meaning of transformation – his personal experience of transformation – would be clear when he could envision what he was doing when he used the word. This was a crucial understanding in our work together; it wasn't enough simply to know the word intellectually, he needed to have a relationship with it, it needed to live and breathe for him.

Scott sat still for several minutes before he finally spoke. When he envisioned the action of transformation, he realized the action he saw was love. But he felt uncomfortable using that word because he thought it was a cliché – "everyone wants love." I reminded him that if love was his word, it didn't matter if it was anyone else's. He had to choose the word that was right for him.

Love is always transformative, Scott explained, but if he was more specific, the word that he kept returning to – the word that felt exactly right – was Compassion. The image that came to mind when he considered transformation was a Scott who moved through the world, free of self-hatred and pain, transforming lives by showing great compassion, that the act of transformation for Scott is to be compassionate. This seemed incredible for a man who was obviously so hard on himself, but when we examined Scott's life, it was clear that he was known by others for being compassionate most of the time. Whenever he chose not to be compassionate, it was almost always at a time when he feared getting hurt. He went into self-protection, rather than towards where his beauty lay.

I asked him for examples, and he told me about his ability to talk to anyone, the fact that people often trusted him on the spot and often told him their life-story, anywhere from train stations and airports to bars. When I asked him to go back further to childhood, he told me stories about the kind of boy he had been with other children. A good friend credited Scott with helping him at a critical point when he had considered suicide. Scott was compassionate at his core, even though his protection against pain often shut this compassionate side down in his adult life – mainly towards himself.

I explained to him that whether he was a "successful" artist by the world's standards or not, transformation is who he innately was and compassion was the path to reach his beauty. In other words, Scott would experience his beautiful life when he learned that compassion – both for himself and for the world around him – was his truth. Transformation would occur in his life, not because of a great effort to transform but through simply being compassionate. Compassion was his purpose.

"I thought my purpose was to be an artist," he said.

"That's your vision, your career. Your purpose is compassion. Being an artist can get you a good job but relating to your art through compassion will transform the world."

Scott was quiet for a very long time. "Most of my life I've felt like a failure," he acknowledged. "I know what you are saying is true. But I haven't felt myself to be that person in a very long time."

I told him that he had never stopped being that person, even if he had forgotten who he was. Compassion was what he was fighting to receive from the world, when it was really what he needed to give to the world. At our core, we embody what we are searching for in the world to feel complete, only to find it within.

Scott left our session with homework. I asked him to go out into the world "consciously following" his purpose, showing compassion to himself and others. When anxiety lined his face, I reassured him, "You can't fail at this, Scott. There is nothing to achieve. You're not inventing anything new. This is about beginning to learn and understand more about you. Just do what you do with intention, but this time ask yourself, what does compassion look like in each situation?"

"I'm not sure if I can."

"It's your purpose, Scott," I reminded him. "It is who you are and have always been. You don't have to search for it anymore, your choice now is to reveal it. By choosing to practice compassion, compassion will find you."

When I met Deena for coffee months later, she looked radiant, and I told her so. The tangerine summer dress she wore complemented her skin, and her hair was shorter. I thought of her walking along her beach in her visualization and realized that a tension which I had come to associate with her seemed to be released. We found a table by the window and sat down together in the streaming sunlight to discuss her third or purpose word.

In the months that followed our earliest sessions together, we'd discovered her third word, Empathy. By receiving her second word, Vulnerability, and meditating on it, and bringing vulnerability to her experience of her first word, Power, she was able to realize that the deepest expression of her power was found in her ability to empathize with others.

Initially, like Scott, Deena had expressed doubts. Power, as she had always defined it, had very little to do with empathy. It wasn't the first word that came to mind when she thought about power – in fact, in the circles in which she had always travelled, it was usually the last. People destroyed their empathy in her industry in order to appear more powerful, and here we were looking to empathy to lead her deeper into power.

"That's the beauty of it," I told her. "Remember, we're not looking for a textbook definition of the word. We can find that anywhere. The third word in this process is definitely not one-size-fits-all. We're looking for your personal expression of power. What does power personally mean to you? This will return you to your purpose."

That conversation had led us to several others. She was able to acknowledge that while "ruthless" power often got the job done in her work, it had never personally fulfilled her. But her second word, vulnerability, helped her to see that empathy for others was the action she needed to learn to feel powerful in the world.

That afternoon, in the coffee shop, she shared that she'd been looking for opportunities to empathize with others, and that had led her to a desire to volunteer more of her time. As an exercise, I'd asked Deena to think of someone who was doing what she imagined she might do in the world. Deena mentioned Audrey Hepburn, a hero of hers, and the fact that Hepburn, in her later years and her second "career" as an ambassador, was, in many ways, the embodiment of Deena's two words. No longer beautiful in the "ingenue" way of her early years in Hollywood, Hepburn enjoyed a different kind of power in her seventies, and part of that beauty came from her service to others. For Deena, focusing on Hepburn was an important reminder that one can serve at any age, when the voices in her head told her she was "way too old" to make a life change.

We talked about what empathy looked like for her; how the action of empathy appeared. What did empathy look like as it manifested in the world, for her. As we discussed the possibilities, a childhood memory came to mind. She recalled her senior year in high school. She had confidence and power, and felt it was one of the last times her empathy had truly been in action. As a peer leader, she volunteered to take a new girl around and introduce her to the other students. The girl, who had moved from France in her senior year, was depressed, intimidated by her schoolwork, and had trouble adjusting. Deena tutored her, helped her get involved in school activities, and they became close friends. The girl's grades improved, and at graduation her parents came and thanked Deena personally. It was a simple memory, but an instructive one.

Empathy, her third word, finally had a context: she had a sense of what empathy in action looked like – loving and supporting others. Empathy was the way in which Deena chose to express her power in the world. It gave her a feeling of satisfaction that was deeper than just "getting the client" or "closing" or making money. Power might mean all those things to someone else, but what mattered most to Deena was to see someone on the other side of her care.

*At our core, we embody what
we are searching for in the
world to feel complete, only
to find it within.*

Deena explained how she was often shamed for her empathy in the past: she once told a friend that she wanted to volunteer for the Peace Corps and was told she'd never make any real money by devoting herself to causes. "You can't fix the world," her mother told her. "Just take care of yourself." But her feeling of power from an early age told her she could indeed fix the world. In fact, that's all she wanted to do! Coming from a very materialistic family, she was almost ashamed to admit that making money didn't matter too much to her. In fact, making money was easy. Money wasn't the issue in her life, feeling connected to her purpose was. This was where her third word would act as her guide.

"Look to your purpose," I told her. "Empathy is your action. When we take this third word and apply it to your life, we understand that it isn't enough for you just to achieve at work. You have to make a difference in people's lives. There has to be an emotional connection if you're involved or you won't feel powerful. That isn't true for everyone's definition of power, but it's true for you."

"Sometimes I'm afraid that I've been shut down so long, I don't know how to empathize anymore," she admitted. "I've had this crazy idea of going back to school to become a therapist. I'm just afraid I'm going to make a fool of myself, I'm scared that opening up like this is going to be painful."

"Living your life without a connection to your purpose is what's been too painful for you," I said. "Most of the time, our purpose, our third word, is also what we've been looking for from the world. You've been waiting for someone to empathize with you, to really see you. Now you have a chance to do that for others. When you get deep into your purpose, you find the greatest pain is not the empathy you haven't gotten in life. It's knowing that you could be of service to someone and you haven't been able to share that empathy with anyone because you've been blocked. We put up all this protection to keep from getting hurt, but the truth is, we're hurt already!" She smiled sadly in recognition. "Protection never keeps anything out, but it definitely holds something in."

We sat together in the silence. "I'm going to try," she finally said. "I'll admit, I'm terrified. But no matter how long it takes, I'll find the right opportunity to reveal my purpose."

"A lot of people think that their purpose is a job they have to go out and seek. Empathy is who you are," I reminded her. " If it is truly your third word, then every moment is a chance to live your purpose. Most of us feel we need a great opportunity to reveal who we are. But your deepest sense of purpose will never be attached to a job or career, because jobs come and go."

As Deena learned, your opportunity is always in the present moment. Right now! Go into the world, committed to being your beautiful self. When you are in your beauty, the opportunities you are looking for will find you. Every interaction you have is a chance to empower through empathy. Empathy doesn't begin when you find the right place or person or organization. It begins when you remember who you are.

Gretchen came for a session with me because she was frustrated and exhausted with trying to find a new relationship. When she arrived, I took in her silver bracelets which clinked like musical instruments when she gesticulated, the enormous oversized turquoise ring, and the hint of gardenia. Gretchen needed no encouragement to talk. She knew exactly why she was there, and her dark green eyes stared powerfully into mine as she began her story.

Gretchen had recently experienced a very difficult break-up with a boyfriend she'd been with for years and had hoped to marry. Having taken a long break after Chris, she decided recently to start dating again. Her sister had suggested on-line dating sites, and she said she'd give it a try, even though she wasn't convinced it was her style. Friends also attempted to drag her to nightclubs and parties. Reluctantly she went, but she found the experience of dating exasperating overall and, most of the time, humiliating.

"Sometimes I go out with friends and several people are interested in talking to me," she explained. "Or I'm online and people respond to my profile, and that feels good."

She ran her hand through her thick brown hair and sighed. "Then the next day, no one seems interested, and I feel totally worthless. It's like I'm on the stock exchange, and I never know whether my value has gone up or down that day. I don't know what to do about that feeling. I do know it doesn't feel good."

I began, "Well, the first thing I would say about that is –"

She interrupted, smiling. "Don't ever date again? I'm already a step ahead of you."

"I wouldn't go quite that far, although that might seem like one way to solve the problem." We both laughed. "The feeling you're describing," I told her, "is very important, as is your example of the stock exchange. In the end, it doesn't matter whether a date or partner made you feel special one day and unimportant the next. That's outside of you, the part you can't control. The experience we are looking for comes from within."

Gretchen's two words were Healing and Trust, and her third word was Joy. Her purpose, which she admitted she'd known intuitively all her life but rediscovered through our work together, was bringing joy into people's lives. Joy was the way that she experienced being a healer. While other people might have described Healing, her first word, as being nurturing, or showing great acts of kindness or selflessness, Gretchen had always been clear: healing, to her, just meant having fun. Sometimes her parents considered her partying "frivolous", but she knew intuitively the true healing power of having a really good time.

This was one of the reasons Gretchen had helped plan and decorate most of the dances in high school, why she was always the one to throw surprise parties for friends in college, to make cakes for co-workers on their birthdays, and organize the baby showers for all her girlfriends. Just to see that look on a friend's face when everyone yelled, "Surprise!" or when a girlfriend opened her shower gifts, made Gretchen happy. And there had to be music, bright colors, good food and drink, dancing and, most importantly, laughter, or the party wasn't complete.

After her relationship with her boyfriend ended, Gretchen retreated from experiencing joy in her life, allowing others to plan the parties in her absence. She not only stopped planning parties, she declined most invitations, often staying at home by herself. Now she was going out again, and, according to her, the results were disastrous.

"Let's start with what we already know," I said. "No matter what other people think about you, you are who you are, no matter what. That's what we always want to return to. You always have to be okay with you first. Remembering your purpose will get you back in alignment."

"I hear and understand the words, but I can never figure out how to tell my heart."

"I understand, Gretchen. Think of it this way. It's not the other person who validates who you are, even though it is very tempting to perceive it that way. We don't know what 'they' are thinking or feeling, we have no control over that. What we do know is that your purpose is to bring joy. No matter what happened with your break-up with Chris, that hasn't changed. And it never will."

"Well, I sure as hell don't feel very joyful right now," she replied. "What am I supposed to do, just fake it?"

"You are trying to get to the innate truth, where your love exists, where beauty resides. It's not enough that you go out to a club and all the guys are into you. That might be a nice feeling, but it's not the feeling we're after. The feeling that you really want is to come home knowing that you were true to your purpose, regardless of what others said or did. That is where your light comes from. When you truly know that, you radiate a confidence that is hard for anyone to resist. And you will attract someone who is connected to his joy, when you are fully committed to yours."

"It seems so clear, talking about it here. Out there, I feel overwhelmed. But I will admit, there was one time, recently, when I had to travel for work. I sat next to this guy on the plane. He was so easy to talk to, and we got on the subject of break-ups and divorce. He is remarried now, but he knew exactly what I was going through and he gave me some very loving advice. It was a beautiful conversation."

"And how did you feel?"

"I felt completely aligned. I probably will never see him again, but I felt so much joy when I got off the plane."

"For the nine guys that don't get you, the tenth guy will," I assured her. "And you need to stay in your beauty and stay attuned to who you are, so you don't miss the experience. You don't need to run after the other nine, taking a poll to find out why they don't see you. That's their business, and trying to control them is about fear, which is never attractive. What you know to be true, before you even walk out the door for the date, or for work, or for any experience, is that your purpose in the world is to bring joy, and that's where your commitment lies, even if it is only joy for one person – you. You'll see, your entire experience with relationships will change."

"Promise," she said. She didn't wipe the tears.

"I promise, Gretchen. The truth is – the person you need to be dating right now is you."

When Scott arrived at our next session, he barely sat down before he began. "Something happened with my compassion homework, but I'm almost embarrassed to share it with you."

"Nothing is too big or too small when it comes to purpose," I reassured him. "I'm interested."

"Well, I did what you said, I tried to show more compassion. Nothing extraordinary, but just in little ways. And I was kinder to myself. I told myself, you don't have to cure cancer here – just go into situations and ask yourself, am I being compassionate, like you said, and then see what happens."

"Perfect."

"So, I held the door open for someone, and said good morning. I felt that would be a compassionate thing to do because he was holding several packages. I even smiled. And this guy walked right past me and didn't say thank you. Not one damn word. Like I was a servant. I was so furious I wanted to kick him. I wanted to shout, 'Hey, Buddy, I'm not your damn doorman.' I was furious most of the day."

"I see."

"What's the point of being compassionate and sharing my purpose if I'm just going to get walked all over? I'm not signing up for that."

When Scott calmed down, I said, "It's not the other person who validates who you are or what your purpose is. What's happening right now is that you've gone into protection. That's how it works with most of us and our purpose. You've had an experience where you now feel you have to protect yourself. You showed your purpose and vulnerability and felt harmed by the response you got back. So now the temptation is to think, 'I can't be me, I have to become something else to get what I want. I have to become hard.' But that takes you back to your conditioning. Not only is there no beauty shining at that point but to be 'hard' you have to abandon your purpose altogether."

"So, I'm supposed to let people just walk all over me? Is that it?"

"No, you're not. But what you're doing now is trying to control that person's response to your compassion. What we know from what you've described is this: as a compassionate person, your concern is being compassionate. You are looking for the compassionate experience, including for others to be compassionate towards you. But then when they are not, you immediately shut down and go to a place of protection."

"I felt ashamed."

"But when you think about it, Scott, the shame wasn't yours, it was his. You did a compassionate thing for someone. Why should you feel shame because that man was rude?"

"It was humiliating for me. I know it's childish. But in that moment, the first thing I thought was, 'I'll never open a door for anyone again.'"

"This happens more and more as we get older. There is a connection to this story and to what happened to you as a child. What you did for that man was a lot like the kind of boy that you described to me, the child you were before you shut down. That was a time in your life when you were vulnerable, willing to help others. But at some point, through disappointment and shame, you began to look to the world to validate your purpose, to tell you that it is okay to be who you are. So, when the person doesn't say thank you, or slams the door in your face, it makes perfect sense that you might say, 'See? I can't be compassionate because this is what they will do to me when I am', even though we both know that the experience of compassion is what you want in your life more than anything else. You're looking for someone to show you compassion, when you are compassion. Do you see the difference?"

"I'm not going to run around opening doors for people like a fool just to fulfill my purpose, if that's what you mean."

"Just pause for a moment and let's examine what happened." Scott shifted uncomfortably in his seat and frowned, but I could see he was listening. "This person who didn't say thank you basically ruined your day. He became the stronger party and had authority over you. This is actually a great example you've brought here. I know you thought this was an insignificant incident, but it is a perfect representation of your life."

"In what way?"

"Your inner self is compassion. In that moment, by holding the door, you were presented with a choice. He doesn't say anything, what do you do? What does compassion want to do in that moment? Your monitoring his reaction to determine who you are is you working from the outside in rather than from the inside out. It's not coming from a place of truth. So what follows is another conditioned pattern that reveals itself the next time you want to be compassionate. You go into the world looking for the person who will automatically shut the door and not acknowledge you. Now you're angry and hurt and so when someone else tries to show you compassion and love, you can't receive it because you're still in your protection mode from the guy who didn't thank you."

"I don't like what he did."

"You don't have to. But if your compassion required his response, then it wasn't real compassion. It was manipulation."

"Manipulation? How?"

"Your compassion in that moment is conditional. You are only showing him compassion because you are looking for him to show you compassion back. That's not compassion, that's a business transaction. What if he is unable or refuses to show you compassion, but the next person you meet does? Beauty becomes manipulation when the only reason you're revealing your truth is because you're trying to get something in exchange."

"But what if you live in a world that doesn't value compassion?"

"That doesn't change your purpose. You're still who you are. When you're not honoring yourself, you put the other party in charge. When you are aligned with purpose, the reaction of others doesn't matter. And it's not enough to say, 'Well I don't give a damn what he thinks!', because that reaction is defensive; it is still coming from pain. I'm not encouraging you to be a phony, or to pretend it feels good when someone doesn't say thank you. What we're talking about is your experience with compassion, regardless of what that man said or did. The question is, "Can you still have a compassionate experience, can you remain in your beauty, even if someone else decides not to make a beautiful choice?"

I continued. "If you really want beauty in your life, there is no negotiation. Just because the world is choosing to be ugly, doesn't mean that you can't be in your full beauty all the time. And what you did for that man was beautiful. Isn't that enough?"

"I didn't consider that. I just stopped feeling anything after I felt hurt."

"If you withhold your purpose in the world because he doesn't say thank you, then you're the same as him," I explained. "Like attracts like." You're trying to move your energy to the higher vibration of love. If you move to energy that is not loving because he didn't say thank you, you're putting him in charge of your life. That man was mirroring back to you your old pattern. The temptation is always there, to revert to our conditioning. The decision to revert to your conditioning versus standing firm in your purpose is always yours to make, not his. There is a possibility in every moment to discover a new approach, to extend beyond our conditioning. You can prefer that he say thank you, but the minute the conversation only becomes about how he reacts negatively to you, he holds your power hostage, the experience becomes ugly, and all your power is gone."

"I didn't feel very powerful, that's true. I was pissed off all day."

"You were within your glory in that moment, in that act of kindness when you wanted to help him, until you let go, not when he let go. It wasn't about his thank you, Scott. It was about your showing compassion when you opened the door and caring about another human being. At that point, regardless of what he did, the experience was complete, your purpose was fulfilled."

Scott nodded. "I think I'm seeing this. Go on."

"The goal is to be able to have an experience in life without constant protection, to be sensitive and vulnerable, and open. To know in each moment that I am okay with who I am. Security is always within the self. Which means not relying or depending on something else or someone else to save you.

"This is the work. Every step you take towards your true self, it may seem as if you are confronted by something or someone else in the world that tries to stop you. But you have to stay with it. You have to say, World, this is who I am! I am going to be compassionate no matter what 'they' say or do. How can I live in fear, when I know in my heart I am compassion? That question will lead you to where your beauty lies."

The goal of Truth of Beauty, and its only goal, is to release what is holding you back from being your most beautiful self. When you discover your third word and acknowledge your purpose, a wonderful change in your life begins.

Knowing your purpose doesn't mean the work is complete – the adventure, in fact, has only just started! The shift from living unconsciously to living your beauty each day increases with greater degrees of awareness and commitment. Once you have identified your purpose, you will find that life brings you many opportunities to find out how committed you are. These opportunities, while sometimes challenging, allow us to clarify our intention, and remind us of our truth.

As I shared earlier, my third word, my purpose, is Care: learning how to care more for myself and for others. Several months after I discovered my third word, I had an experience in which I felt very uncared-for by a friend of mine. We had made plans to get together, I was ready at the appointed time, and my friend cancelled at the last minute. He didn't speak with me but wrote me a text saying he couldn't honor our plans, which I received as my hand was literally on the door to go and meet him. His reason for canceling was not an emergency, which I would have completely understood, but because it had slipped his mind, and now it was late, he was tired, and said, dismissively, "let's just do something some other night". I should also mention that this had happened before. I found myself feeling taken for granted. My conditioning from the past told me to shut down, to lash out at him in anger, or to call someone we both knew and complain about what he'd done. But I knew that wasn't caring for me or him, and with my commitment to purpose, I had to ask myself, What was the caring thing to do in this situation?

Conditioning may not only dictate how we react to people, but also the way we perceive entire situations. I knew the victim in me wanted to see this experience as another example of someone letting me down. I had trusted, been vulnerable, was excited to see my friend, and now look what happened! The temptation was real in that moment to choose resentment and not to consider my purpose at all.

But I knew there was another option. Perhaps this experience was sent to me so that I could have a deeper understanding of care, so that I could really put my new understanding of purpose into action. It is one thing to acknowledge one's purpose intellectually, but quite another to apply it in situations in which you feel uncomfortable, angry, or hurt. I tried to see the invitation I was being given, and how I might come through this experience even more caring than I'd been before. I'm not going to pretend that this part of the process is easy. The time I took in that moment was essential; if I'd just picked up the phone and called him right away, he probably would have been speaking to my conditioning. I had to remember that if being cared for was important to me, then I needed to bring care into our experience together. I was going to commit to being caring to both of us, regardless of how angry I felt. But first I had to ask myself what caring looked like.

Before I called him back, I checked my alignment. I'll be honest, I was angry, and so this step didn't just take an hour – I had to sit with my feelings, on and off, for a day. Feelings of abandonment have been a real trigger in my life, which is part of the reason why "care" is such an important word for me, and such an essential part of my purpose.

Being true to my purpose meant that first I had to focus on the experience I was having with his behavior, and then explore what caring meant from that place. My responsibility, and my only responsibility, was to care in that moment by sharing my truth. To insist that he adjust his behavior in order for me to feel better, or to issue an ultimatum - you change from now on or else! - wasn't caring for either of us and would give him authority over my experience.

If you really want beauty in your life, there is no negotiation. Just because the world is choosing to be ugly, doesn't mean that you can't be in your full beauty all the time.

I spoke with him a few days later when he called. I was genuinely happy to hear from him because he is very important to me. I explained to him that I valued our relationship and shared with him how I felt about what happened. I also shared what commitment meant to me. The goal wasn't to change him but rather to see if we were enrolled in the same vision of friendship – if we were aligned in our expectations. If not, neither one of us had to be wrong or "the bad guy", but that was information we needed to know going forward, whatever the result.

This was powerful growth for me because, unlike the past, I hadn't ended the friendship on the spot, or ignored his calls for weeks, giving him "the silent treatment" until he got the message – the old patterns of protection. Or – another conditioned response – ignored the behavior completely because I was scared to lose my friend.

Now, by being closer to my personal truth, I not only felt strong (Strength being my aspirational word, the word I chose to empower my first word, Beauty), but I knew that, no matter what his reaction to what I said, I had honored my purpose. I do know he felt cared for in that moment, because we discussed it later. He admitted to me that he had a pattern of standing up friends and sabotaging relationships – part of his fear of commitment and of being loved – and had lost several friends as a result. I was one of the few people who had been completely honest with him and hadn't tried to change him. Our friendship is more beautiful as a result.

From the examples you have read in this chapter, you have the tools to discover and describe your purpose. If for any reason the process feels overwhelming, or you find yourself feeling a great deal of doubt, always return to Trust. When you feel you have sufficient trust in yourself, continue your exploration of Purpose.

Remember: your third words is always about action. What do you see yourself doing when you consider this word? Be as specific as possible and take as much time as you need. What's most important is that the word should resonate with your soul. When the exercise is complete, you should be able to say, "That word absolutely describes who I am."

Be aware that this process can open us up to greater levels of vulnerability. With the many people I have worked with, Describe is often the place where some find themselves feeling exposed and experience this step as a little scary.

The reason why fear comes up for us is that, by identifying our third word, and thus acknowledging our purpose in the world, we begin the process of real change and commitment to our beautiful self. The paradox is that in actuality we aren't really "changing" at all but returning to that which we know ourselves truly to be, before the experience of pain and protection encouraged us to lead a life ruled by conditioning and away from our beauty and purpose.

Once you know your purpose, and begin to tap into the power to carry it out into the world, you discover that your truth and your power are not beholden to the circumstances you find yourself in. From this clarity, it becomes almost impossible to feel victimized because there is no one to blame. You become entirely responsible for your own happiness. For some people, this produces a sense of panic, because on the deepest level, the search for self outside oneself ends, and part of our conditioning is also being addicted to "the search". By acknowledging our purpose, we find that often what we have been looking for outside ourselves to make us whole, we've had all the time.

Try not to abandon the process. Be gentle with yourself and appreciate the courage you've shown to get this far! Your entire world changes when you no longer look for yourself in the world. Knowing your purpose, and committing to it, instantly puts you in perfect alignment with who you are. The rest becomes practice. When we know what our purpose is, our relationship to the world, to others, and to ourselves is transformed.

The next step, Visualize, allows us to use our purpose and imagination as tools to create the beautiful life we want. I am asking you to appreciate this new understanding of your purpose not as a confrontation, but as an invitation to greater self-knowledge. When you step into the world with an awareness of who you are, your energy vibrates at new levels and the world has to respond. As I tell my clients at this point in our work together, you have no idea of the beautiful path that lies ahead.

Visualize

The purpose of the outside world is to reveal to us who we are.

We test our experience of purpose through the fourth step of Visualize. It has been my experience, as I have worked with hundreds of clients over the years, that Visualize is the crucial turning-point in the Truth of Beauty process. Sometimes, however, right after people have mastered the step of Describe, I notice them begin to back off. What should be a point of great relief and excitement at knowing exactly who you are and what you really want, becomes a source of anxiety. We may recognize consciously for the first time that we have not been allowing ourselves to be ourselves, and that realization can be painful. What we may not be able to see at first is that this understanding, however difficult, is also the crucial step that leads to a place of real transcendence.

In order to experience a full relationship to our beauty, we must be able to visualize it in the world. Visualize, in this context, is not only about what we want to see manifested in our lives, but, more importantly, how we have learned to perceive life in the first place. We are often taught that if something is wrong in our lives, we must look outside ourselves: this usually gives us a reason to begin blaming others. In Truth of Beauty, we make a different choice: we know we must examine our negative conditioning in order to live fully in our truth.

Not all our conditioning is bad; some of it is, in fact, extremely useful. For example, as children we are taught to look both ways when crossing the street, or to say thank you when we receive a gift or compliment. The conditioning I am referring to in this chapter is the pattern of behavior we have created in response to the fear of being who we are. We will return to conditioning many times in this book because of the ways it keeps us asleep to our power. Appreciating the power our conditioning has over us leads us to truth by allowing us to examine our assumptions. Our conditioning is always familiar, but it will never give us the answers we need, and, most importantly, by the time we reach the step of Visualize, it will no longer protect us.

Deena once described the process of facing her conditioning as having the blankets snatched off you when you're sleeping at night and the house is freezing.

When I asked her what she meant by this analogy, Deena told me that she felt "naked" and "exposed". What I heard behind her words was that, for the first time in many years, she felt vulnerable. The analogy is an apt one; we've been snuggling up to our conditioning for years, like a safety blanket, and we now have to risk being a little uncomfortable in the process of "uncovering" our truth.

In my sessions with clients, I often hear people say they are not able to live their life "out loud" because when they do, they get hurt. When they live "exposed", they bump against pain again and again, re-affirming the belief that they have to suppress who they really are or learn ways to protect themselves. This protection is high and, as we get older, it only gets higher, like a wall, keeping people out, and keeping us locked in. But at some point we have to test our beauty in the world. Eventually we discover that it isn't beauty that hurts; it's the conditioning we've developed to protect our beauty against those experiences we fear will harm us.

Facing your conditioning may bring on a temporary identity crisis. If you take away the conditioned belief system, a distorted relationship to self that you've nurtured and invested in for years, you may feel like you are "out there", "left hanging" or "empty" – phrases I've heard in private sessions. The reason for this is that you haven't yet arrived at a consistent experience of practicing your truth, the beauty you are still developing. This is when we need to trust the process the most.

How can you tell if your life is ruled by conditioning? You feel angry and exhausted. As the years pass, we are frustrated at not being able to be who we are, and we run out of people to blame. We gravitate to others who share our conditioning. We can continue to participate in this "cover-up" or we can return to a place of trust and ask the question: who will I be when I stop listening to my conditioning and uncover my beautiful self?

The experience of going deeper into your truth means risking being vulnerable all the time. It recalls a time earlier in life when we were open to the people around us. No one is more vulnerable than a child who wants to love and be who they are. This is one of the reasons that we begin with trust and memories from childhood; it is also the reason that for some people this step in the process makes them want to run for their lives. It is easy to see why many find it easier to go back to their comfort zone – their conditioning. In some cases, we've invested in a life based on conditioning for twenty, thirty, forty years; it's what we know best. Our conditioning is familiar, a song we can sing without even thinking about the words, like "Happy Birthday" or reciting the alphabet. It can rule and ruin our lives and we don't even know the impact it has on us every day because we just see it as our way of life. It takes courage to slow the film of our life down so that we can examine it frame by frame and see how our thinking and choices contribute to our unhappiness. Visualize gives us this opportunity.

With the step of Visualize you are taking your beauty and testing it in the world. If your experience of beauty in the world – and by the world I mean society, the workplace, romantic relationships and families – has been one of feeling harmed, this may be the last place where you want to be vulnerable. It's more familiar to go back into protection and defense as the answer to pain; and on some level that definitely works – some of us may even consider that strength. We navigate these choppy waters our entire lives, going back and forth, with beautiful moments here and there, usually followed by a return to our conditioning. Being ourselves in the world can be akin to celebrating a holiday; it comes around a few times a year, but it's a special occasion and not a daily way of life. And it doesn't lead to a transformative experience or ultimately fulfilling your purpose. Visualize reveals that it is impossible to be in your beauty and in your fear-based conditioning at the same time; ultimately, if you are committed to being truly beautiful, you have to make a choice.

In the Truth of Beauty context, we use the idea of visualization in a unique way. Often, we are told that in order to manifest what we want, whether it is a new car or a new relationship, we need to focus on it exclusively to make it happen. Many clients I've worked with were confident that if they could only get a new job their lives would change. While that type of visualization can create results, we've all known someone who got exactly what they thought they wanted, and months or years later they still weren't happy. Their desire, and eventual disappointment, just led them to want more things.

Now, to be clear, there is nothing wrong with wanting things. I chose a career in beauty and fashion because I love beautiful things! The difference in our work is that beauty and visualizing don't stop there. Visualize in this context is less about what we want from the world, and more about who we are in the world. With Visualize, we see ourselves and our choices, and observe what the world is giving back to us as experiences. If something happens, rather than blaming everyone else, which is how we're often taught to respond, we ask, "What role am I playing in this?" And, "How are the choices I'm making in this moment keeping me from living my truth?"

Through the step of Visualize, we begin to apply to our lives a type of vigilance, an unflinching look at the areas where we are hiding behind a façade – the mask we wear that keeps us from revealing our beautiful self, a mask that we developed through conditioning. Visualize is a powerful game-changer. Once on board, you no longer envision your life changing because someone else modifies his or her behavior. Change depends upon your willingness to see exactly who you are and what you bring to the world in each moment. When we are able fully to visualize who we are, we are able to move on to Acceptance, the fifth step – seeing others as they are.

When we are fully in our beauty – we can have what we want materially, we can enjoy it and we feel we deserve it, no longer held hostage to the kind of attachment that says, "If someone takes this away from me – the money, the cars, or the relationship – I'll fall apart." We see that the material things we want may enhance our lives from time to time, but – and this is essential – they no longer have the power to define us.

The reason why many of us continue to lead stagnant lives is because on the deepest levels we are terrified to let go. We won't let go because we don't know any way to live other than with control and fear. We're scared to change because we think it's going to be painful, and who wants more pain in their lives?

We don't get to our beauty through pain; we get to beauty through truth. Pain is sometimes part of the process; but it doesn't define us, it informs us. We use the past as an entry point – we are only focused on our history when it ultimately leads us back to beauty. Exploring our pain has value when it moves us to the truth of who we are.

When you know your purpose in life, and you go out in the world fulfilling that purpose, you are beautiful. Visualize helps with that process.

In a powerful follow-up session, Scott and I returned to his earlier experience of holding the door for a stranger and discussed his recent frustrations with work as well as a petty argument with a family member. The specific details of what was happening to him weren't as important as the fact that Scott was exploring a new way of responding to his life. He was examining all his experiences from the viewpoint of Compassion. Through the process of Visualize, Scott was able to see when he was his compassionate self, when he was fulfilling his purpose, and also when, out of fear, he returned to his conditioning.

Scott found that the more he trusted himself the less he felt like a victim when dealing with other people; he felt more authentic. There were still those people in his life who he feared weren't ready to appreciate his "new" compassion, but he found there were others who were very much open to it, even if they were complete strangers.

He shared a story with me; he was in an airport, and a woman serving him at a coffee bar gave him a smile that was so open and generous, he was taken aback. He smiled too. "I know it sounds stupid," he later told me, "but I felt as if she had shown me a part of her soul. The whole exchange couldn't have lasted more than a few seconds, and then she said, 'Have a great day'.

"And I know it wasn't about flirting, or anything like that, it was deeper. It was so strange. I've had people say 'Have a great day' a million times, I've said it myself and usually don't think about it, like a reflex. But somehow the way she said it, I felt like I'd been wearing sunglasses indoors my whole life and I'd taken them off for the first time and really looked in someone's eyes. Corny, right? I said, 'Thank you, you have a great day too,' and I left. I know I may never see her again, but I won't forget that moment. I really saw her." I told Scott that he had practiced the step of Visualize perfectly; and the woman had mirrored back to Scott his purpose in the world.

I said to Scott, "You are compassion. Any time you walk into a situation, you are assessing if you can be compassionate. In the past, the focus of your energy wasn't about compassion, but rather about protecting compassion, or protecting yourself from being hurt. Remember, the easiest way to know you are not in alignment is this: whenever you are defending yourself, you are in your conditioning. True beauty doesn't need protecting from anyone."

The only reason we ever protect ourselves is because we are trying to get to a place where we can truly be who we are. Deep down you hope, as we all do, that one day you will be able to live your truth without being hurt. We learn early how to protect, to be other than who we are. We then keep re-conditioning ourselves to be the exact thing we really don't want to be. We may think we are outsmarting the world, but we are only outsmarting ourselves. You are a child when you start this cycle. By the time you are an adult, you know the game well. It's like an actor who has always played the same part in a touring company; you can do Hamlet in your sleep. After a while you may feel you can no longer differentiate between the actor and the role.

In my own Truth of Beauty process, I came to a startling revelation about the past: at one point in my early life – and I couldn't remember exactly when it started – I began to lie. I lied about everything, and the more you lie, the more you have to lie. I'm not talking about lying about your taxes, or to your romantic partner about cheating; I mean lying to myself and others about who I really was. As far as beauty was concerned, lying meant I was hiding.

After a while I began to forget what I was hiding, and it felt as if the world was totally against me. In my mind, I was just trying to "make it" and get what I wanted, but the world became more superficial because my entire focus was on the outside world. This is the reverse of the experience we are seeking in Visualize; I was looking to things and other people to make me feel beautiful. I thought that having things of prestige would gain me access to the world that I wanted to be a part of – in other words, if I had the amazing house, the designer clothes, the right car, I would be acceptable. As I've said, there is nothing wrong with wanting or having any of these things, but I wasn't approaching them from my purpose of caring, but from desperation and fear.

I'd completely misunderstood Care, my purpose word, because as a child I wasn't allowed to acknowledge who I really was. I was thrust into protection from a very early age: several relatives I lived with reacted with impatience and violence after my parents died, and my experience of caring openly was cut off way too soon. I only became aware of this later, when I went to my earliest childhood memories to get behind the lies to the truth. For most of us, the truth stops very early in our lives – you may be fortunate enough to pinpoint it to a particular incident or to a year in school. It is essential to figure out when you stopped living your truth.

What we are trying to determine is when the lie came into your life, which is the condition; when you became the condition; and why you felt the need to perpetuate it. I could tell in my sessions with both Deena and Scott that they found this part of the process and the language I was using uncomfortable – no one likes to be called a liar, and personally I hated admitting it to myself. I eventually had to stop lying because it was no longer working; it was bringing me unhappiness, and I just kept having to lie. I finally said to myself, "Let's try to be really honest and see how that works." I knew that to be honest, I had to begin with exploring my need for protection.

Visualize reveals that it is impossible to be in your beauty and in your fearbased conditioning at the same time; ultimately, if you are committed to being truly beautiful, you will have to make a choice.

The majority of us are living in protection all the time. We are always on the defense. It's almost a reflex, regardless of the experiences we find ourselves in. Having healthy boundaries is important, but protection for someone like Scott meant going into the world as if wearing a sign on his back, "I know you are eventually going to hurt me; it is only a matter of finding out where and when." By focusing on his purpose, Compassion, we were able to consider that perhaps it was the habitual pattern of choosing protection that was causing him pain, rather than what anyone was actually doing.

Later in our session, Scott described something that had happened to him during the recent holidays:

"I was in a drugstore in Times Square buying wrapping paper with several shopping bags in hand, and I put them down briefly to pay and then left. The store was packed, the streets crowded, and I just wanted to get home. I reached the subway, and there was a woman there asking for food, and I walked past her to go down the stairs when I suddenly realized I'd left my most expensive gift on the counter, a piece of jewelry I'd bought for a good friend. I nearly panicked. I ran all the way back to the store, and it wasn't there. I'd only been gone ten minutes, but it's New York. When I asked the cashier if she'd seen it, she said that she knew I'd be back and she'd put my gift in the office for safekeeping. I can't tell you how relieved I was.

"When I reached the subway entrance, the same woman was standing there, still asking people passing by for food. I am always afraid I'm going to get ripped off in these moments, trying to decide if people are lying or not – I don't want to be a fool. But I felt so good about my package, like someone had smiled on me, and I wanted to say thank you. So, I said to her, 'I'd like to buy you dinner.' We went to a nearby restaurant and I bought her a take-out meal. She said thank you, and as I paid for it, I looked at her face and thought, 'I would have walked past her before and just gone home if I hadn't gone back for my package. I was in such a hurry, fighting everyone in these stores, to get what I wanted.' She thanked me again, and I saw how much she appreciated this act of kindness. Meanwhile, I felt ashamed for being so suspicious before, when it was clear that she was in serious need. What I paid for that meal wasn't even a tenth of what that gift cost."

"Why were you so afraid of being made a fool of?" I asked him. "What you did was very compassionate."

"I figured you were going to ask me that," Scott said and smiled. "I thought about it all the way home. I remembered when I was about nine, a kid at school asked me if he could borrow some of my allowance for an emergency, and I trusted him, so I said yes. He promised to pay me back but he didn't, and when I asked him about it, he said, 'You gave me that money as a gift", or something like that, and that he was never going to pay me back. I was so mad that I told my father, and he said it was one thing to be a fool with my own money, but I wasn't going to be a fool with his; he worked hard and money didn't grow on trees. I didn't get any more allowance for two weeks. I was so ashamed. I hated that feeling; every time I saw that kid, it felt like someone had kicked me in the stomach."

I asked Scott more about where the belief system that "people rip you off" came from, and he told me, "From my father. My father was always angry about work, he always felt taken advantage of. I felt guilty that he had to work so hard, my mother too, to support us. I just remember the word 'sacrifice' coming up over and over again. He was always looking for a new job because he was so toxic and bitter no one wanted to work with him."

Talking about Scott's father gave us insight into Scott's conditioning; for Scott's father, with rare exceptions, compassion was weakness. And it was his father's voice Scott heard, a voice that had now become his, when he went through the world trying to negotiate whether or not to make a compassionate choice.

Scott and I explored what it meant to be in protection; the same compassion he had shown the boy at school, he had shown the woman at the subway. But he had learned from the boy and from his own father that compassion leads to hurt and shame. When Scott was awakened to his purpose, the experience of almost losing his package interrupted a pattern, or rather, let down his defenses so that his compassion could emerge.

The challenge presented to Scott in Visualize was whether he could maintain being one hundred percent compassionate and stay fully in his beauty, totally committed to purpose, regardless of how the world responded. His conditioning would always remind him that "people are out to get whatever they can, and if you aren't careful, they will run right over you. You have to put yourself first." But that wasn't where his truth would be found, and being cynical in order to avoid being humiliated wasn't his purpose.

The experience of fulfilling our purpose is rarely black or white. Most of us have moments when our beauty shines through regardless, when we express our purpose here and there and experience wonderful results. But too often this is fleeting. For example, we choose to be compassionate around other compassionate people when the stakes aren't too high, or in very special circumstances. That's very different from a commitment to purpose that says, "Regardless of what 'others' do in the world, I will remain in my purpose at all times. Period. Not because of anything I want or need to prove, but because of who I am. I am the experience I want of my purpose in the world."

In these decisive moments, the step of Visualize brings us to a life-changing concept: instead of constantly assessing and asking the world for permission to be who we are, we exist from truth and let the world adjust to the purity of our intention. Remember: the purpose of the outside world is to reveal to you who you are. Through Visualize we are able to see how our purpose is being reflected through our life experiences. This isn't about blame for the times when we are disappointed. It is about constantly assessing whether we are clear in our intention and appreciating what life is showing us in that moment.

Scott's instinct to explore his relationship with his father, in order to understand his feelings about compassion, was right. He had to go back to where he had been fully trusting and where trust had "failed" him, where he'd abandoned compassion for protection. When I first presented Scott with the possibility of being compassionate one hundred percent of the time, he looked at me as if I were out of my mind. "No one can be that vulnerable," he told me. "Everyone will walk all over you." But when I reminded him that there had been a point in his life when "compassion" was so natural it wasn't even a word to be memorized or defined, but a natural part of who he was all the time, he looked close to tears. As we looked back on the trajectory of his life, Scott discovered that as he got older, through grade school, high school, and college, he had become more protected each year. For Scott, as for many of us, protection often meant choosing to be alone.

Showing compassion for others had become defined as an energetic interaction, one that involved the risk of being vulnerable followed by what occurred when Scott wasn't protected: disappointment. The reason conditioning is so strong for us, and why challenging it can be so scary, is that it is locked up with our earliest memories of our parents, or other people we love. We don't even realize we are acting out their scripts rather than having our own fresh, unadulterated experiences.

We may become so suspicious of everyone that we create relationships in which we are consistently disappointed. If we don't get the disappointment we are looking for, we may meet new people and draw it out of them. Because this is what we know and believe to be the truth, the people we choose in our life will often accommodate this pattern. This isn't about blame or excusing other people's abusive behavior. Sometimes we find ourselves in relationships where the best way to honor ourselves is to walk away. But when we find that we are having a similar experience in the world repeatedly, the process of Visualize demands that we examine what we are putting into the world as a result of conditioned expectations. It is possible not to blame circumstance, and yet still explore our energetic relationship to it. This is part of the process of discerning which experiences are part of our purpose and worthy of us, and which we'd like to leave in the past. If we only respond from our conditioning, we stay in reaction mode, creating the same destructive relationships over and over again.

If your conditioning is doing the thinking for you, you may decide to get rid of friends and isolate, because interacting is too painful. Or people sense your constant defensiveness and may leave in frustration. Whichever way it works, once that process takes off, your relationship to the world becomes a battlefield.

Scott and I concluded our session by returning to the woman he had helped on the street. I asked him if there had ever been a time where he had chosen not to help someone in this way. "Yes," he replied. "A man asked me for help three weeks ago. When I tried to do the compassionate thing and offer to get him something, he wasn't interested in any of the places nearby where I could buy him food; eventually he got very angry when I didn't give him the money to buy something himself. He seemed drunk or high. I had a feeling about him; I wasn't comfortable with that, so I walked away."

"How did that feel?"

"I felt guilty, like I'd let someone down, but ultimately, I felt I did the right thing."

"So, in that moment, the compassionate choice may have been to say 'no'; compassionate to yourself, and maybe to him."

It made sense from Scott's history that his first thought would be, "Is this person trying to rip me off?" "What am I going to get in return?" "Am I going to be made a fool of?" While these were significant questions, and perhaps even accurate ones – maybe this person did want to rip him off – I asked him to consider the most important question: "What is the compassionate choice in this situation?" Judging the individual or himself for the behavior was just part of his conditioning. We cannot commit to beauty and be judgmental, especially in situations where we are still trying to understand how to apply our purpose, where we are trying to learn.

There would be times, I explained, when someone might slip through the cracks, where he might get ripped off, have his feelings hurt, or someone wouldn't accept his compassionate offering. But what was most essential was his unwavering commitment to purpose; to his truth.

Committed to purpose, his clarity would also attract the people who were as compassionate as he was, and that's what he wanted. I assured Scott that as he began to trust more, life would present him with the compassion he'd been looking for: it would have to, because he would find it all the time now – in himself.

One reason we love the archetype of the superhero is that when things go wrong or there is danger, while the natural human instinct may be to run in the opposite direction, the hero rushes towards the situation and asks, "How can I help?' The hero knows her purpose, where her strength lies. For Scott, his commitment to Visualize meant walking confidently in every situation and asking, as he did when he bought the woman on the street a meal, "What does compassion look like here?" "How can I transform this moment through compassion?" We may feel the need to initiate great campaigns before we can act from purpose, but, as Scott discovered, a life can be beautiful by linking one small compassionate act to another through the day. As *A Course in Miracles* says, "All expressions of love are maximal."

I'm sure you remember, as I do, being a young child and playing outside with your friends. Usually at some point, someone fell down and got hurt, and said with pain and accusation in their voice to another person in the group, "Hey, you did that on purpose!" We often think of something being done on purpose in a negative way; but what would life look like if you did everything on purpose, but for your greater good? Not just falling into circumstances, like someone who can barely swim falling off a boat into choppy water, constantly coping just to get through each day; but rather, living in a place of strength, knowledge and clarity – doing everything on purpose every day of your life with intention?

The transformative response to fear is being fully present; in the here and now. Being present is to be fully in purpose, being filled with gratitude at the process and for the freedom to express ourselves truthfully is to experience illumination.

There is a built-in temptation that we constantly face in Visualize, especially at the beginning: if the world doesn't see or acknowledge our purpose, we may feel like shutting our purpose down, like a show that closes after one night of bad reviews. Vulnerability gets shut down right along with it. The result is that we are in the world, but technically we are no longer available. We're stalling, waiting for our beauty to find us. Too many people I've encountered exist in this place. They are living in the world and doing what they need to get by, but they aren't experiencing happiness; and life feels like something to endure, requiring forbearance, rather than a dynamic way of being. Or they decide the only way to get what they want is to fight.

One client I worked with recently, Lilian, explained when we got to the step of Visualize that she was tired. She would sometimes drift off while we were talking about her purpose. The first time she said it, I thought she'd just had a long day at work, or a bad night's sleep. Eventually, she said it so often, I began to realize she was tired of living, tired of fighting, that she wanted to check out. The phrases were familiar. Sometimes you will hear people say, "I'm getting too old to change", "I'm set in my ways", "I'm close to retirement", "What's the point anyway, everything stays the same", or other expressions. Usually they are just variations of "I'm too scared to be beautiful." I didn't believe that Lilian was suicidal, but rather that she was frustrated. Knowing her story, I wasn't surprised.

Lilian came from a family that valued education; she herself had attended a Historically Black College, and her first or foundation word was Classic – she loved anything that was classic, from cars to vintage fashion to family heirlooms. One of her favorite possessions was an antique set of pearls given to her by a great aunt. Beauty to her meant representing herself in a classic, conservative way; her clothes and hair often reflected a fashion sense that would never date itself. Her third word, her purpose in life, was Inspiration, and she dreamed of being a mentor to younger women. She had a great admiration for women in history whose contributions had led to change. In order to realize her first word, she felt she needed to be more Confident – her second or aspirational word. Lilian grew up in a religious family, in which she was constantly competing with a younger sister who got most of the family's attention. She worked hard all her life but never felt "seen" by her family. As a gay woman, she believed that some of their resistance was based on their shame about her sexuality. Even at fifty, she resented that her parents still favored her younger sister, and she'd reached a point where she felt she wanted to give up. Part of her frustration lay in her constant feelings of failure: how could she inspire anyone else, if she couldn't even inspire her own family to support her? Many of her workplace scenarios only emphasized this same rivalry, as she got passed up for promotions for women she was competing against.

It is possible not to blame circumstance and yet still explore our energetic relationship to it.

Lilian made a decision in her forties to really fight, become more aggressive; but that wasn't her energy. The decision led to some benefits, but increasingly Lilian felt a sense of frustration and failure, and now she was exhausted. Our work together would be finding a way through Visualize to help her see her value without needing her family's approval. She was already playing a role in community activism and inspiring others, but because only one person's approval really mattered to her, her mother's, she couldn't accept any of it, couldn't see herself. Wrestling with her beauty had worn her out. Lilian promised to come back for another session so we could explore her family in more detail.

I'd like to emphasize here: we can get some great results from fighting the world. Some people are amazing fighters; they fight their way through life, they fight their way to transformation, they fight for love, for power, for resources. Every day is a battle and they are up for it!

Fighting definitely works, it may even get you many of the things you want. The problem is that it eventually numbs you out. And you may find yourself alone. People who fight all the time – and I've known some famous fighters – may achieve their goals, but once their talent leads them to abundance and all the things they dreamt of, they are shocked to discover they can't receive any of it. Having abandoned vulnerability along the way, they aren't really there, to appreciate the abundance life has given them. They can stand at a podium and wave to the crowds, but when they go home, they don't feel a thing.

Some of these people may even be familiar with their purpose without doing this work, but there is a lack of integration: their purpose is hovering above them, somehow detached. They have achievements, and occasionally fame, but they aren't really present for any of it, nor are they present for the relationships in their lives. They are so busy fighting, they never stop to ask any of the critical questions we are asking here: how do I engage with my purpose, not just to acquire things or recognition, but to have a beautiful experience with my entire life? Years later, an emptiness sets in; the fighters don't have to fight anymore to get what they want, they have everything. And yet they don't understand why they still can't be present in their lives.

For those of us who have been in the beauty industry for a long time, we have a special blind spot. The experience of being aloof, above it all, remote, can be very seductive. She's not in pain, she's a "diva". He's not fighting for his life, he's just "fierce". Personally, there were times when I was shut down to myself and my purpose, but I pretended not to care. People were afraid to approach me because I appeared arrogant and detached. This only contributed to my isolation and moved me further away from what I really wanted – to bring beauty into the world, to fulfill my purpose, Care. But being shut down wasn't caring towards myself or towards anyone else. It only added another layer of protection, another reason to fight the world to get what I wanted.

Visualize requires us to give up fighting completely, which is why some people get frightened at this point – they hate the feeling of being defenseless. When we choose to stop fighting to be who we are, the noise in our life diminishes long enough for us to ask a penetrating question; why am I fighting for something I already have?

In the fourth step of Visualize, transformation comes from the realization that we have the power to change our lives forever when we surrender to purpose. Take a moment to really appreciate what your purpose word has meant to you in your life, and how powerful, and occasionally painful, your relationship to this word has been. From this experience of concentrating on your third word and integrating it into your thoughts, begin by examining your choices throughout the day. How do you see this word interacting with your daily experiences?

We are on a mission here to trust who we are and be honest with ourselves, to understand ourselves better and the choices that we make in every given situation. Some of my clients have found it helpful to keep a journal at this point, to record the times when they feel frustrated or challenged, but also to acknowledge when they have a beautiful interaction with someone, when they feel fully aligned with their purpose. Aligning with our purpose, by the way, doesn't have to mean that we successfully reach all our biggest goals. You may remember Scott's interaction with the woman in the airport coffee shop. Some of our most beautiful interactions may take place in a few brief moments and with people we never meet again. What defines these moments as beautiful is not how the world perceives them but how you think and feel about yourself.

Visualize completes our basic foundation and leads us deeper into the second half of Truth of Beauty, where we will explore deeper levels of integrating our beauty into the world. With a new appreciation that our purpose cannot be diminished or harmed by any circumstance or opinion, and with a renewed commitment to bringing that purpose into the world, we find we can only be led back to our birthright and a place of true happiness; where we are empowered, living on purpose, and ultimately free to be ourselves.

Accept

Vogue editor and legendary fashion icon Diana Vreeland once said, "The strong face comes not only from the bone construction, but from the inner thinking." In the fifth step of Accept, we take a closer look at our thinking and how it affects our beauty. Examining our thinking is another way of saying that we go deeper into the process of committing to our truth.

We all intuitively know that when we face the truth of who we are, when we commit to purpose and stand in our beauty, everything in our lives will change. Acceptance is a life-changing decision we make about how we choose to relate to the world. While the word acceptance at first glance may seem passive, it is actually where the action begins!

We have located our beauty through our third word and seen its potential through the process of Visualize. Acceptance takes the experience of realizing our beauty from theory to daily practice. It is the beginning of fully experiencing your beauty not just from time to time, but as a consistent way of life. With acceptance, your beauty depends on nothing else but your commitment to living fully from your truth. When we accept full responsibility for our beautiful experience in the world, we no longer have to fear that our "beauty will fade" or that someone will take our beauty away from us. In short, our beauty is no longer conditional. We no longer catch ourselves thinking, "If only he would do this, or if only she hadn't done that, then I could really be my beautiful self."

Acceptance, in this context, ultimately leads to complete authority over your own life: we are empowered because our beauty is no longer dictated by our circumstances or the behavior of others. Beauty is responsibility. We all know what it is like to feel sad or disappointed by another person's behavior, to be stuck in resentment and anger over how we feel someone has affected our choices. But when there is no one to blame anymore, a different type of sadness may set in at first– followed by a new clarity. We now have to ask ourselves a powerful, life-challenging question: "Why am I afraid to be beautiful? What am I holding back in this moment that is keeping me from having the beautiful experience I desire?"

This way of thinking is very different from how we are taught to live in the world. Too often we are encouraged to lie, to blame, to cover things up and to live behind a façade each day, even when we are aware that our lives aren't working. We are taught to react to the world; what the world says about us is how we define ourselves. When we don't get what we want, or we aren't fully in our power, we blame the person standing next to us. Acceptance defines the psychological shift that says, "I choose to live in my beauty now. There is nothing and no one to wait for or that I need to complete me or my beautiful experience. In this moment, I accept that I am enough."

To accept our beauty in the world means that our relationship to our life has to change fundamentally. The only way to reach this place is to drop our mask – the identity we've created to protect ourselves from pain. Once we begin to see the role we play in the negative situations we create, we can deconstruct them, move through our unhealthy conditioning, and change our relationship to our lives. I can be vulnerable, truthful and, finally, myself. We often take for granted that we should just know how to be ourselves but knowing yourself is a process – it takes work. On some level, what we are doing in the fifth step of Acceptance is unlearning the process of being who we taught ourselves to be for others' approval rather than who we really are. As a client of mine said recently after a discussion on childhood fears and following her purpose: "It takes courage to stand in your truth."

For such a basic, simple word, Accept is a revolutionary, transformational moment in our Truth of Beauty work. Think about it: when you fully appreciate that your beauty is not conditional – no longer based on the behavior or approval of others – you stop looking for your truth externally, you stop asking the world to release your beautiful self. True beauty needs no permission.

Before we continue, I believe it is important to make a distinction here between what is true and what is truth. I remember listening to a lecture by author and metaphysical teacher Caroline Myss several years ago in which she said that while something may be true, that doesn't mean it is truth. I found this insight to be extremely helpful and the key to this fifth step. In Truth of Beauty, we acknowledge the fact that there are situations we may not be happy with, and while we may understand the circumstances to be true, that doesn't mean they define the truth of who we are. Accept helps us to understand this crucial distinction.

A client of mine, Martin, had a friend Daniel with whom he shared a difficult, combative relationship for years. While that statement was definitely true about their relationship, Martin became aware that whenever he was fighting for power with Daniel, he was not honoring his truth. Martin had to accept the fact that his relationship with his friend was difficult – which was true. But in order for him to transform his experience with Daniel, which really meant with himself, he had to go deeper into truth. What is true in a challenging situation – that we feel unhappy or angry with someone – may tempt us to try and change the behavior of others; truth, on the other hand, is to know that we can't change anyone. Truth always returns us to the Self.

Orlando, an activist and organizer, shared with me that he feels guilty seeking to be beautiful when the world is such a mess and so many people are suffering and living in pain. To him, committing to his beauty is vanity, a waste of time. He encounters situation after situation where he feels too powerless and angry to make real changes. His fear is that he will one day die unhappy and unfulfilled. Orlando feels he needs the entire world to change and be at peace in order for him to be beautiful and to live his purpose. When I pointed out that there are approximately 7.6 billion people on the planet, all of whom would have to agree in order for him to be in alignment with himself, he laughed.

I told him, "While it is true that many people are suffering in the world, and we must accept that as true, that isn't the truth about who people are, what their potential is. You've shared with me that you believe that the world will one day be a beautiful place and that people are inherently gorgeous. That is your truth. We just haven't gotten there yet. Stand in your beauty now, Orlando, and lead us there."

As you read the stories in this chapter and observe my clients' sessions, be aware that there is a critical dialogue taking place in all of them, and also in you. It may feel sometimes like a debate, a shouting match, or even a war. We are constantly trying to communicate with our deepest truth, trying to find an answer within ourselves while moving beyond negative conditioning, and often, in moments of difficulty, we feel hopeless or stuck. It is a profound act of self-love to stay committed to this process, even when it feels confusing, scary or new.

I've had a range of reactions from clients when we reach the step of Accept. Some are depressed, others anxious, a few get angry, and one client shouted out with great relief and tears in her eyes, "I knew it all the time, I can't change anyone but myself, but it just helps so much to hear someone else finally say it out loud!"

None of these responses is wrong, of course; I've experienced versions of all of them myself. What is happening here, along with our empowerment, is a process of letting go, a loss. To be clear: acceptance does not mean resignation. Just the opposite, in fact – we have more control, not less, to make changes in our lives when we accept a situation and can examine it honestly. How can we respond with purpose and truth to a given situation if we are afraid to see what is true?

Dropping our control, which is what acceptance means, is also the end of trivial pursuits; in other words, the interpersonal power games and petty grievances that grind us down and disempower us day after day, but also make us feel self-righteous and justified for staying stuck in our relationships. Acceptance eventually means a full-on confrontation with our belief system – not theirs, but ours.

When we challenge the negative conditioning that we've used for years to explain to ourselves why we can't be beautiful, we may begin to recall all the times we've compromised our truth in order to get love or approval. It might have been a family member or a partner who suggested, "I'll approve of you when…" We waited, we turned ourselves inside out, and the approval never came. The further we go into acceptance, the more we begin to see that our negative conditioning leads us to repetitive and addictive psychological patterns, encouraging us to seek the same type of approval we wanted in the past, and usually getting the same disappointing results. When beauty is something we must attain from others, it also becomes something we can potentially lose.

In other words, when the question "Why won't you – family, husband, boss, world – allow to me to be beautiful?" suddenly changes to, "Why am I afraid of living fully in my truth?" there must be a radical shift in our lives. This is the challenge presented to every one of us: will I choose to stay with what is familiar, even when I know it ultimately won't get me what I want, or am I willing, no matter how frightened I am, to consider there may be another way?

Equally important, we must accept ourselves and our personal timing during the learning process. Going into situations in which we used to blame, criticize and defend as tools for coping, and responding now with acceptance, may seem strange and unfamiliar at first, not unlike focusing on a neglected muscle at the gym. You will get stronger. Remember: we are always seeking to get to our truth, but often that authentic voice is hard to hear because our conditioning competes with it or drowns it out. The practice of acceptance brings that conflict into our awareness so that we can examine our life experiences in detail. When we are fully in acceptance, we are led to the ultimate realization that there are no circumstances in which we are unable to fulfill our purpose in the world. You are fully responsible for your beautiful life.

Corrine, who loves to cook for her friends, is usually on the phone when I arrive for dinner. She has a demanding schedule and catches up on her calls while she is preparing the meal. I don't mind as I know I will have her full attention when we sit down and eat together. On this occasion, she waved me in as I took off my coat and walked into her apartment. I complimented her on her printed dress, chain-linked necklace and a combination of silver and gold bracelets. Her shoulder-length hair was tucked neatly underneath a patterned matching scarf and her flawless skin with just the right amount of make-up looked as if she were going out for the evening. I admired the perfect place settings on the dining room table with fresh flowers in a glass vase as the centerpiece.

"Do I have the wrong day? You must have a big date tonight!" I teased her.

"Yes, but he's no one special," she said, smiling. "Sit down, it's almost ready."

After I petted her Pomeranian, poured the wine, and made myself comfortable on the sofa, I overheard her talking to a friend about a female colleague at work whom she "just couldn't stand". She described her frustration in detail, and how badly the woman had behaved at a recent staff meeting. This wasn't the first time I'd listened to her on the phone speaking this way; she'd had similar conversations about men she'd dated, female friends who couldn't be trusted, and family members who'd betrayed her. The conversation usually began with, You won't believe what she, he, they, did today....

Corrine is a very attractive woman physically; she takes great time and care with her appearance at all times and I've often overheard people call her "stunning", like a supermodel. I share this here because being seen as beautiful by others has never been Corrine's concern. She knows she looks good because she works hard at it – as a performer she feels it is expected of her. But she has also expressed a disconnection in her life, that she doesn't always "feel" beautiful, and that often her life seems adrift. That evening at dinner, while discussing a challenging period in a romantic relationship, she asked me about my Truth of Beauty work. This led us to a conversation about acceptance.

I honestly shared with her that while I'd always been deeply impressed with her talent, I'd observed that her beauty seemed to be withheld somehow, on hold too often because of people around her who she believed were behaving badly. In other words, she wasn't taking any responsibility for her experiences. I could immediately tell Corrine didn't appreciate this insight. Her defense was that the people around her were always behaving badly, that's why she had to keep them in line. The problem was, I explained, she could never relax; defending herself had become her full-time job. As soon as she straightened one person out, someone new came into her life to disappoint or frustrate her, another person who needed "correcting." Even though I personally knew several people who loved her deeply, she had a reputation for being "highly strung", "neurotic", "over the top", and that meant that she was often in conflict with close friends. At times, this left her alone and bewildered, especially since her first word was Radiance, and her third was Nourish.

Several aspects of Corrine's life communicated a deep inner warmth, from the way she cooked to the colors she wore and her gifts as a performer. I wasn't surprised that Radiance was her first word when I first heard her sing. And I could confirm her third word was Nourish after having had dinner at her house! Her second word, Patience, is what she often felt she lacked when dealing with others, especially in her romantic relationships and at work.

When Corrine was pleased with life, she "fed" the people around her, nourishing them both physically and spiritually. The issue in her life wasn't whether or not she could experience joy occasionally; the problem was that she didn't feel she could be fully nurturing in most situations, because, truth be told, Corrine never felt nourished herself. Someone else's behavior always determined whether she could be in her purpose at any given moment. I explained that was the same as deciding whether one should go to graduate school based on whether it was raining outside. She needed to find the place in her where she could nurture herself and others, experiencing true joy in her life, regardless of her conditioning or other people's behavior.

Corrine explained that being on stage released her, she was always connected to herself when she was singing. Yet she was also aware that in those moments she was on stage alone. To fully experience Radiance in every aspect of her life meant being nurturing, sharing and helping others to feel supported – particularly with a life partner, which she wanted badly. From our earlier talks, I was aware that Corrine felt abandoned in her childhood and had a lot of rage about that. Being physically beautiful had ensured that she was taken care of by her family, that she was "wanted", even if it meant that she sometimes felt exploited for her talent and good looks. She was noticed whenever she was "on" and performing, and then soon after she was neglected again – no nourishment there. Now, in her forties, she wanted to create joyful spaces in her relationships in order to feel fulfilled, to give freely and lovingly to the people around her, but too often somebody came along and enraged her. The men she met would stay around for a while, impressed with her talent, but when she didn't feel like impressing them and being "fabulous" anymore, when she needed to be held and taken care of by someone, they disappeared. Just as in her childhood.

Staying angry was her defense against pain from the times in her life that her trust had been violated. We had to go to a place of vulnerability for her to bring forth her third word, Nourish, and to appreciate how her negative conditioning was getting in her way.

Using the step of Accept meant that in our conversation about beauty and purpose, we weren't allowed to begin with what her co-worker had done to her that day, or how she felt about the man she had recently broken up with. We both knew there were many places she could go for that conversation, but that it wouldn't lead to lasting change. And while we needed her childhood history to explore her early conditioning, we weren't allowed to dwell on that either. Ultimately her beauty had to begin and end with a decision that only she could make – the decision to live in acceptance. Accept, as a tool, would reveal to her through her daily interactions with others whether or not she was living from her purpose, and would affirm: your beauty can't exist when you are trying to control everything. Surrender. Accept what is true in each situation, and then examine how you are tempted to respond from your negative conditioning. When you are aware of your patterns, choose instead to go deeper into purpose.

The change you are looking for begins with you. The world will take care of itself.

Lilian arrived at her session enraged about a conversation she'd had that morning. She was dressed elegantly, as usual, in a navy suit and with her dark glasses. In our months of working together, we had discussed her experience with her immediate family, growing up in the black church, and the rivalries with her sibling that I outlined briefly in the chapter Visualize. She'd shared several stories with me about her frustration with her younger sister, Marie, but I had never seen her quite this upset before.

I offered her a tissue and waited while she wiped away the tears. "I'm sorry," she said. "I feel so stupid crying. And after all the work we've done. I know I shouldn't let Marie get to me. I felt I was doing so well before, and now this."

"You're exactly where you're supposed to be, Lilian," I reassured her. "When you're ready, tell me what happened."

"We're planning an 80th birthday party celebration for my mother," she began. "It's going to be a very big deal, including members of my mother's church, some of the college students that she's taught over the years and our extended family. I thought, This time, I'm going to try and really work with Marie. No fighting. I will ignore her selfishness and control and just focus on my mother because it's her special day and that's what matters."

"Sounds great."

"I actually wanted to take the lead on the project, especially when I thought about my third word, Inspire. And I felt really inspired, for the first time in a long while, to take charge. I even had an inspirational theme just for the younger people at the event, a short video – I wanted all of my mother's grandchildren to share what her life's journey had personally meant to them. I had a total vision, and my being in charge as the oldest in the family felt right. As you know, Marie is usually the one in charge.

"So, I told her my ideas and we agreed to divide up the responsibilities. We made a list of each of the things we were going to do, and a week later when we checked back in, everything I did, of course, was wrong for some reason or another. Then I found out later that she went behind my back and spoke to all the people I had originally called, just to make sure I'd done everything 'right', meaning, of course, her way. I felt humiliated and undermined. When I confronted her about it, she said she just wanted to make sure things were going 'according to schedule' because there was a lot at stake, and everyone knows how I put things off."

"Was there anything else that bothered you about the call?"

"Oh yes, I forgot to mention, she also asked if I was bringing someone, implying that I shouldn't invite anyone too flamboyant because it might embarrass my parents. She didn't use those words exactly, but she's used the word 'discretion' before because of our church community and our extended family and our parents' friends who still don't know I'm gay. That's the word she uses when she wants to say something homophobic but doesn't want to seem hateful. I was so angry when I got off the phone. I came this close to hanging up on her and letting her do it all, which was probably her plan when she started the fight in the first place. And the entire event was my idea!"

"How do you feel now?"

"I'm hurt," she admitted. I handed her a cup of herbal tea and she thanked me, setting it down on the table between us. "She has no right to tell me who to bring. But I realized today I feel shame. She's not completely wrong about my planning, I have procrastinated over things in the past. Paying bills, missing opportunities. My family used to tease me about being lazy as a child and I hated it. I don't believe I was lazy, I think I was depressed. But things were going to be different this time. I really tried. Marie knows if she keeps frustrating me, I'll back off, then she will get to do it all, and when the time comes, she'll also get all the credit. She is so manipulative."

"So why are you here, Lilian?"

"Because I have no idea what to do! Usually I would have called her back and shouted at her, but I knew I'd say something I'd regret. I didn't want to do that this time, but I don't know what else to do. I'm completely stuck."

"The reason why you are stuck," I offered, "is because you know there is a new way to approach this situation, even if you aren't fully there yet. When you reach the step of Accept, it can sometimes be very important to do nothing.

"I'm glad you didn't call Marie back just yet. This is a time to reflect, to examine the situation as it is presented to you. The old way, as you've described it, is to rush in, guns blazing, and just react, and you and Marie get to have one of your famous fights. But that doesn't feel good, that feels ugly. You have different tools now. You know your purpose in the world is Inspire, and inspiration is how you bring your first word, Classic, into the world."

"What if she doesn't want to be inspired? I know I don't feel very inspirational at the moment."

"That's because you are fighting with your conditioning. You have a history with your sister, and a history of how you've reacted to her. You're tired of arguing, right?"

"I'm exhausted," Lilian admitted. "It's the same battle, with variations, that we've had since we were children. And I'm always the one who has to say sorry to her. But not this time."

"So, you don't want to fight her, but at the same time you're worried that you'll be letting her 'get away with murder' by apologizing to her. It's either fight or flight. You're deep in your conditioning."

Lilian sat upright suddenly. "I know it sounds crazy, but for all our battles, I really hate to fight! One time I tried just to agree with everything she said to keep the peace. I only did it because Mama was sick that year, and she hates it whenever we fight. My parents always took her side, even when we were kids. I feel like I'm about six years old right now, telling you this. Anyway, it didn't change anything, she still found a way to criticize me. I felt like a doormat and a fool and eventually I just had enough. We didn't speak for almost a year."

"So, there is a third option here, Lilian."

"I'm listening."

"The third option is that you don't run away and you don't tell her off. You stand in your truth. You accept her and the situation. Right now, you are looking for a working solution where she changes her behavior so that you can be happy. The answer you're really trying to find doesn't have anything to do with managing her, but everything to do with managing yourself. Because your ultimate goal is to be at peace with yourself. You want to feel good about you. You want to be in your beauty no matter what your sister says or does.

"Because of the negative conditioning, the temptation is to make it all about Marie's behavior, to say to yourself, 'When she finally changes, then I can change.' You've been waiting for that for over thirty years. You are the change you are looking for. It's not up to you to change another person to make you happy. You can only change yourself."

Lilian sighed heavily and allowed me to continue. "It is valuable for us to process what happened on the phone. But we aren't going to focus on Marie. It's not about Marie, it's about you. So, what do we know? We know that you and Marie trigger each other, which is true. But only when we stop attaching your experience of beauty to Marie's behavior, can we get to your ultimate truth. Accepting the situation means acknowledging your sister's behavior towards you. Marie behaves in a way you find controlling. That is true. But that's not your truth. We have to look at the conditioning that keeps leading you to this same place with her."

*Your beauty can't exist
when you are trying
to control everyone.
Surrender.*

"I don't know how to do that," she admitted. "I feel so angry."

"Well, let's start with your bringing someone to the event. It sounds like your sister has some issues with your orientation, which may be true. But you know your sister's opinion is not your truth as a gay woman, right?"

"I never made that distinction before."

"You must. And you also know you can't change Marie. You may find it hard to stop your negative conditioning from coming up during your interactions with her. We can never get rid of our own negative conditioning completely. But we can acknowledge it is there and choose to challenge it. Then, once we are in awareness, we make the decision to go deeper into our purpose. The conditioning may rear its head from time to time, but you decide with acceptance that your purpose is stronger. It will always be your guide; it will never let you down. Your third word, your purpose, is Inspire. So, you have to ask yourself again, what does Inspire mean to me? What does it mean to me in this moment? What would it feel and look like?"

"When I think about the women who inspire me, I think about their power and commitment. They don't let pettiness get in the way. And they've had much bigger adversaries than having to plan a party or deal with a younger sister like Marie."

"Go on."

"When I think about Classic, my first word, I keep seeing a woman with composure and power, a woman who handles herself with grace. Beautifully dressed and with great style. But it's not just fashion. It's courage. Poise. Refinement. None of the things I feel about myself at the moment, even though I can see them so clearly. But I feel good just saying it out loud. I feel inspired, actually."

"Does anyone specifically come to mind?"

"I think about Coretta Scott King, she's one of my idols. Rosa Parks, Jacqueline Kennedy Onassis, Princess Diana, Michelle Obama. And I had an aunt, my father's sister, who I adored. She was always dressed beautifully, she was a nurse, and once she took me shopping and we had lunch together when I was a little girl, just the two of us. She made an appointment with me and everything and asked if I was free that afternoon. I was six. She bought me a little purse, a dime-store kind of thing, not very expensive, but I was so happy. I carried that little purse everywhere, and I was always looking for little things to put inside it. I'd sort of forgotten about that. I know it sounds like a mixed bunch, but those are the women I envision when I think of the word Inspire."

"Perfect. What else do you see?"

"I guess I see a woman who, no matter what happens to her or what has been taken away from her, is a survivor. She knows exactly what she wants in each moment."

"So, what is stopping you from having your beautiful experience? What you're saying right now sounds very inspiring to me."

"I believe in those women. But in some ways, and I hate to say it, my sister is right about me. I don't always trust myself. I do make mistakes or take too much time doing things. Maybe I am lazy, as she says. That's the part I hate – the part of me that agrees with Marie. The part that felt when we were on the phone that she should be checking up on me in case I do something wrong."

"Fantastic. That's what we want to look at. Because what we know to be truth is that whenever you go deeper into your purpose one of two things will happen: your relationship with Marie will change for the better or you two will move apart because you will no longer be in alignment. Right now, you have in common that you both want to be right. We want to see what is happening truthfully and not lie or pretend. If you honestly face your relationship with Marie and tell the truth about how you feel about yourself, the relationship will have to change. But you can't change her mind. You can only change yours."

"But how? I've thought this way for a long time."

"Going deeper into acceptance means first to accept the fact that you and Marie are both very critical of you at times."

"Yes, that's true."

"Now, negative conditioning would encourage us to have a long conversation about Marie's behavior. To attack and condemn her. You may want to defend yourself right here with me. But there is nothing to defend. I'm not saying one way or the other whether you are irresponsible or lazy. What I am saying is that you and Marie are in alignment when it comes to judging you or she wouldn't upset you like this. Your needing to defend yourself means that on some level you must agree with her. We are not looking to defend anyone, Lilian, we are looking to live from purpose."

"And my purpose is to inspire."

"Exactly. Marie is looking for inspiration just as you are. The only difference is you feel that you need the right circumstances and for Marie to change her mind about you before you can inspire. This isn't about convincing your sister of anything. It is about you realizing that your beauty doesn't begin or end with her or anyone else. When you get on the phone with her, you want to be inspirational in that conversation no matter what she says or does."

"I'm still not sure what that would look like."

"What do you envision? What might an inspired conversation look like? When you lead from your purpose rather than reaction, you will be in a frame of mind where you think differently about the situation. You'll be surprised by what you'll hear yourself say. Just try it."

"All right. I hear myself saying, 'Marie, this event is for our mother, it's her day, and I think we should put her first. And I'd like to take the lead on the event, but not without your support. I think this can be a wonderful, celebratory evening for everyone involved if you and I work together. I feel inspired and I hope you do as well. I've got some great ideas about the order of events and the theme, and I've already made some calls to some of the people I'd like to speak that day. I'm very excited to share the list with you. And I would love it if you would take care of the catering and flowers– you did such a beautiful job at your daughter's wedding. And Marie, I've invited Diane to join me on the day as my guest. She's a very special woman in my life and I'm looking forward to your meeting her. Now let's make some time to meet and go over our plans as soon as you're free."

"Sounds fantastic."

"And just then a little blue unicorn peeks out from behind a rainbow-colored tree and eats cotton candy from my hand." Lilian laughed. "I'll admit, it felt good to say all of that, even as a joke. I've never spoken that clearly to her in my life. She'd probably faint in her kitchen and drop the phone."

"That wasn't a joke, Lilian. That's exactly what inspiration sounds like. That's you when you are in your truth. It's not a fantasy, but the opposite of the negative conditioning. The conditioning is a tool you learned as a child to survive, but now you are an adult, and as an adult you now have to deal with this differently. You no longer have to hide from being yourself in your relationship with Marie – *that* is the fantasy and the stuff of unicorns. That's what's false. And you don't need it anymore."

Lilian reflected at this point and seemed a little sad. After a few moments, she said, "I am imagining the woman who could say all of that. She feels beautiful and confident to me."

"The only difference between you now and the woman you envision is that she accepts her beauty and her purpose one hundred percent. She has to, because when she isn't controlled by her negative conditioning, there isn't anything else standing in the way of her being beautiful. She accepts the situations in front of her for what they are, but instead of choosing to react from fear, she realizes that going deeper into purpose is what gets her what she wants. She doesn't look at the relationship and say, 'When Marie changes, then I can be inspirational'. If there is something missing, if there is a need to be fulfilled in the moment, she goes back to herself and asks, 'How can I be more inspirational in this moment?' 'What more can I give?' 'Am I living from my purpose right now?'"

"It sounds easy when you say it. I wish I could do that in the moment."

"I'm not saying it's easy. Not at first. It's a new muscle, but we have to keep working with it. So, for example, in a situation like this, you ask yourself, 'Where did I get the idea that I was lazy? When did I begin to accept that belief?' Marie is speaking to you about you, but she is also giving you the gift of your own perception. And you know this is true because you are still reacting to it, because it still can still upset you so much. When you no longer believe it, Marie will have to let it go, or you may choose to have a different type of relationship with her. When you accept your truth fully, so will she. She's won't have any other choice. You're looking to Marie to give you your power back, but she never had it in the first place."

"I'd like to try this, but it feels risky. I don't want to lose my sister," she said.

"The truth is, you don't have your sister now, Lilian, if being in a relationship with her means that you constantly have to lose yourself to make it work."

Lilian nodded, dabbing her eyes with a fresh tissue. "I really will stop crying. I promise. It's just it's been like this for a very long time."

"I understand," I told her. "It may feel scary, like a journey into the unknown, because if Marie isn't in charge of you, if she doesn't have the power to stop your purpose, nor anyone else, then you are truly free. Which leaves only one question: When no one else is responsible for your truth, and you choose no longer to live from a place of reaction, how much beauty can you stand?"

Several years ago, I went out for the evening with a good friend of mine named Griffin. That memorable evening was to be a defining moment in our relationship and in my Truth of Beauty work.

I'd known Griffin for years, we'd worked together in the industry, and one of our favorite pastimes whenever we socialized together was to judge all the people who passed by. It didn't matter if we were in a hotel lobby, coffee shop or sidewalk café; we'd talk about each person's appearance and what we felt they should wear. Who the people were didn't matter; we knew we'd never see them again, we just enjoyed being critical and finding fault. I'm not proud to admit I behaved this way, but I am able to see now that the experience I had with Griffin forced me to confront something in myself that led me to a deeper appreciation of acceptance, and my own purpose, Care.

At that time, I was beginning to visualize the meaning of beauty in my life. I realized that what I was doing with Griffin wasn't caring at all; in fact, it was often cruel – the opposite of beauty. And as I continued to work on myself and my relationship to the word Care, I had to acknowledge that something was wrong with this situation and that I couldn't ignore it any longer. Care, what I wanted to bring into the world and what I was always looking for in my relationship with others, wasn't occurring for me in these exchanges. How could I expect to have care in my life if I wasn't caring? It seems like a very simple question, but it rocked me to the core.

Before I reached the stage of Accept, I hadn't asked these questions, or if I had, I'd dismissed them, allowing my conditioning to make my decisions for me. In those days, I chose to believe that there was only so much beauty in the world – a paradigm of scarcity that many of us are invested in – and that if I put down others, then my own beauty would feel validated. But believing that meant existing in fear and competition. We never have to compete when we are in our truth. And my truth always led me back to Care.

In order to be fully committed to purpose, I had to make a decision. I knew I had to move forward. I wasn't sure, at first, how I was going to bring the subject up with Griffin. I was aware that we had rationalized our judgment of others because, as we were both in the fashion and cosmetics industry, it was our "job" to judge for a living. I thought we had the right to be critical, our livelihoods depended on it. But I also knew that if one of the people I was criticizing were to come to me professionally for a consultation, I would never laugh at or embarrass them. I would be caring. So why was I afraid to engage in Care all the time?

I began to ask myself: how long could I stay committed to Care without returning, at some point, to my old fears and conditioning? I could see, through acceptance, that every situation in my life was a teaching tool to remind me that I just needed to care more in that moment. Every opportunity I experienced, whether it was pleasant or not, was a chance for me to go deeper into the experience of Care.

My outings with Griffin were very familiar because they reminded me of home; of growing up and spending time with my aunts. The aunts, my father's sisters, were notorious for sitting together at family or church gatherings and laughing with each other as they criticized everyone around them. If it wasn't one woman's hair, it was another woman's dress, or someone's makeup, or perhaps a marriage on the rocks, someone about to be evicted from their home; it could be almost anything. They formed a tight circle of judgment, and it seemed nothing met their approval or got past their watchful eyes. I have a childhood memory of one of my aunts missing a "session" with her sisters for whatever reason, and while she was gone, I was astounded when I overheard them talking about her! I sometimes wondered what they said about me. This memory came back to me as I sat with Griffin and watched us judging passersby.

There was another memory that came up, much more painful, but also about family as it related to Care: I recalled that as a child, when I was looking to be cared for, my experience around Care often led to pain. Care in my family meant being taken care of physically, being watched constantly and expected to behave and stay in line. If I disobeyed, or even had too much of an opinion, the consequences were sometimes violent. I attached fear to the word Care and developed a personality as an adult that was often shut down, because when I asked for care as a child, I was controlled or punished. This only became worse after the loss of my parents at a very young age. I began to understand, as I accepted these memories as part of my story, why I often anticipated so much fear around Care, and why, through negative conditioning, I had created uncaring experiences in my life like my outings with Griffin. I had created an untouchable façade that wasn't real and wasn't giving me what I wanted. I was starving for care, but whenever I approached care, the vulnerability frightened me, and I stayed shut down.

Moving into acceptance meant that I had to face all the unpleasantness and unhealthy conclusions I drew whenever I tried to fulfill my purpose. When I tried to convince myself that my evenings out with Griffin were harmless fun, I knew better. If I wanted to be fully in my beauty, I had to look at this dynamic. I had to remove my mask.

Often, we approach our third word thinking we know what it means. We may know the definition of the word, but our relationship to the word and the emotional complexities it brings up for us can be much more profound. Committing to my truth meant acknowledging what was true about my experience with Care and where it had led me, while believing that the power of my purpose was stronger than my conditioning. The first step, Trust, became significant in this moment, reminding of me who I had been before I shut down, back when I trusted myself to Care in the world without anticipating censure and pain.

I considered my backstory, without dwelling on it. Even though I didn't like the behavior that had been modeled for me, I knew my aunts weren't to blame for my choices now, nor my parents, caretakers nor anyone else. And while it was true that I had seen a lot of criticism and lack of care, this wasn't my truth. Blaming Griffin for "starting it first" or for "doing it more than I did" was also an easy trap to fall into. Blaming him wasn't going to get me where I wanted to be.

Acceptance meant that I had to be completely honest with myself about the experiences I chose to create. Once I took away any justifications for not being caring, once I cut off all the roads holding other people accountable for my choices, I felt clearer about what I wanted to say to Griffin. It seemed like a small conversation, but I knew it was a major turning-point. I reminded myself that I wasn't responsible for Griffin's truth – only my own. While I hoped he would understand, expecting him to change in order for me to transform meant that someone else had power over my life. And I knew that wasn't a beautiful place to be.

A few weeks later, Griffin and I met again for lunch. It was a gorgeous spring day in the Village, and a man walked by our table. Griffin said something about the man's suit and his inexpensive shoes, and a few moments later he pointed out a woman's torn flowered handbag as she was waiting to cross the street. I told him, "Griffin, I don't feel comfortable judging people anymore. It just doesn't feel good." I could see him take offense, even when I made it clear that I wasn't judging him or telling him what to do. I needed a new experience, I explained, and I couldn't continue to participate in that behavior and be true to myself anymore. I hoped he understood.

Griffin taunted me a little at first and laughed. "Come on," he said, "you know you hated that flowered bag as much as I did," or "Those brown shoes were hideous, anyone can see that!" When I still didn't respond, he chalked the whole conversation up to my being in a bad mood, which is why I had to repeat myself when we met a few weeks later.

This time, when he understood I was serious, he got angry. He accused me of being self-righteous and a hypocrite. I even sensed an underlying fear that he thought I didn't want to be his friend anymore – as I once feared about him. It was almost as if he were saying, If we aren't getting together to criticize strangers, or gossip about our friends, what else is there to do? I reassured him that our relationship was important to me and there were other ways that we could engage with each other, but this was no longer going to be one of them.

I don't want to give the impression here that I never judged anyone again. In fact, soon after our conversation, my criticizing and judgmental thoughts seemed worse, mostly because I was now consciously aware of them. The decision I made about judging others, however, marked the beginning of a new process. I couldn't let myself get away with not caring in any situation. I had to accept the times when I saw myself act in an uncaring way, knowing that caring was my ultimate truth. From that day forward, I began to ask myself in every encounter, "What does care look like for me in this moment?" I knew there would be circumstances that might come up as impediments to my choosing to be caring, but living in acceptance meant they were no longer allowed to stand in the way of my truth.

Griffin and I parted ways that evening, and I knew he was still very angry with me, but I was prepared to have a different experience, regardless of whatever decision Griffin made. Even though it seemed he and I were in conflict, the real conflict, the only conflict that mattered, was the conflict with myself. Griffin didn't know my aunts, and he didn't know my history with my family or of feeling judged. I had encouraged the part of our friendship that centered on judgement based on my history. Once I accepted that, I was able to see that it wasn't me versus him, it was me versus my history – my conditioning versus my truth.

Griffin chose to back away from the friendship for a while, which was painful, I'll admit, but caring for both of us in that situation meant that I loved him and I had to respect and accept his decision. I was aware that by standing in truth, our relationship would either deepen or might fall away, but either way it would have to move in a different direction because, no matter what, I would stay committed to my truth. I congratulated myself for being honest and for making a full commitment to Care. It's not uncommon, by the way, to feel you've made some progress and then the next day feel as if you've just walked off a cliff. Negative conditioning, remember, can be strong and powerful. I found this out when, days later, having committed to care, I had an ugly, uncaring experience that I instantly came to regret.

I was at a popular coffee chain getting a drink. I have the same drink every day, I pay the same price. The young man behind the counter rang me up, the barista made the drink and as he handed it to me, I said, "Excuse me, this isn't supposed to be a latte."

"Oh well, that's not what this says," he replied with irritation. "You're going to have to pay the difference."

I paused for a moment, and said to him in a measured tone, "Why are you asking me to pay another amount?"

I considered the facts in that moment. I'd already paid for the drink. I didn't want a big confrontation since this was my neighborhood coffee shop and, as I was in there all the time, someone might recognize me. I told myself, I just want my drink and then I'd like to leave.

Right away, however, I knew I had walked into conditioned behavior. The "wild animal" of my conditioned response was preparing to come out. I was aware of this because I found myself defending myself immediately before I'd considered my purpose, before considering Care. I watched myself react in anger and knew that was not who I wanted to be, not who I was anymore, and definitely not how I saw myself. But here it was, my negative conditioning, familiar and unleashed. I watched it unfold, like watching a car without brakes rolling down a hill.

One might ask, what does a coffee order gone wrong have to do with being beautiful? It's a good question, but the truth is, it is often the small, daily interactions that reveal our conditioning to us in the most illuminating ways, not just the major schemes and campaigns. And nothing triggers my conditioning more in a given situation, for reasons I've explained, than feeling uncared for.

"I already took care of everything with the young man at the register," I said to him. "I just need you to make me the drink that I ordered and we're fine. This wasn't my mistake."

"I can't make a drink for you that you haven't paid for. Now if you'll just – "

I put up my hand to interrupt him. "This line is very long and I'm in a hurry. I ordered something else and I expect you to prepare that now."

"Now what is happening here," I thought. "I am defending myself and I feel victimized. I'm seething. I want coffee, it's early in the morning, if I stand around anymore arguing with this man, I'm going to be late for work. I am thoroughly in my condition. I'm upset because I can't have what I want, and that feels familiar. In my mind, coming from my history, I'm used to people telling me I can't have what I want. I'm upset because I feel a lack of care. There is no beauty involved here. I say that I don't want to hurt anyone anymore, but in this situation, I'm hurting me. I'm hurting myself because I am choosing to make someone else in charge of my behavior. And I am giving all my power to him the moment I make the exchange about him."

I'm forgetting in the moment that my purpose is to Care, which must come directly from me. Now we have a disaster on our hands. Every sign up to that point has shown me that Care is going out the window. I can feel it. My conditioning, my old familiar friend, is taking over. Our negative conditioning always gives us two options only: defend ourselves or run away. Fight or Flight. In moments like these, our negative conditioning is as familiar as remembering your phone number or address, you don't have to even think hard, it's right there, in the back of your mind, ready whenever you need it. It's the default mode, protecting yourself at all costs when you feel afraid. And what I was afraid of most in that moment was of not being taken care of, a feeling I still associate with great pain.

The barista walked away for a moment, then turned around, spoke to the guy at the register and then returned to me. "I apologize, Sir," he says. "You are correct. It was our mistake."

I leaned forward and told him, "Your apology is not accepted." And then I added, "I am late and I need to leave now. Will you please hand me my drink?"

He prepared the drink, and I took it from the counter, still furious, and walked out the door.

I'd like to be clear here: this was ugly behavior for me. It's how I learned to protect myself; by "letting people have it" – being a "diva" – and I don't like it. Whether I was wrong or right by anyone else's standards, or "justified", I still felt wrong inside.

As I walked down the street, I took a second and had a brief "acceptance" session with myself. What had happened in that moment? I found myself in a situation where I was not getting what I wanted and I wasn't happy – that was true. So, what did I want? I wanted the drink I ordered. I forced myself to go even deeper. What did I really want, what do I always want, more than anything else? I want to feel cared for. That's why I got angry. Because I felt that there was a lack of care. I now had to ask myself why I had expected him to provide care in the situation, since Care is my word. To be cared for, I have to go deeper into truth, deeper into my purpose. The question I need to ask (but which is hard to hear with the negative conditioning shouting in my head) is,

"How can *I* care more in this moment?" I know from truth that caring for me means caring for him. When you are in truth and acting from purpose, there is no separation between "us" and "them", "me" and "you". There is only intention.

I considered throughout the day what happened that morning. I studied that whole scenario as if it were in a textbook with charts and diagrams. Sometimes committing to truth requires that level of analysis. My old paradigm would have been to congratulate myself for a job well done, "Boy, I really told him off!" I might even have called a few friends to complain, and they would have laughed and encouraged my performance.

But I knew that if I chose to applaud myself without going deeper into what happened, an important learning opportunity would be missed. Not only that, but some version of my encounter would happen again at a later point in my life. Why? Because this was still who I was. I'd been trying to move past being uncaring and to live from purpose, but this experience revealed to me that a lack of care still existed in my consciousness. The lack of care I'm focusing on here was not the barista's behavior, but the response I chose in reaction to what happened in that moment. What became obvious to me was that I was triggered the minute I felt uncared for, I was losing power in our exchange as soon as I responded to that trigger. That was information I needed to know. Acceptance meant I had to explore why that trigger still had such a profound effect over my life that it could cost me my beauty in any given situation.

In other words, studying what happened that day didn't mean finding a manual on how to deal with rude people, or tips to avoid having your coffee order made wrong. I studied me. I looked briefly at the barista and the choices he made, but my focus mainly stayed on myself.

I replayed walking out of the store, believing on some level that I was in control. There was only a small group of people around, so I wasn't too embarrassed by what happened. I got my drink in the end. But I felt so much anger over that cup of coffee. What I observed about myself was that a confrontation like that could still put me in survival mode so easily, defensive and raging, because I wasn't being cared for. All that old anger and resentment from childhood was still ruling my life. It wasn't about the barista anymore, or about coffee. Now it was about what kind of experience I wanted to have in the world.

The bigger question now became, How do I manage situations like this in the future? Because they will continue to happen until I no longer lead from conditioning but from my true self. How do I avoid going deeper into reaction and fear? And why do I choose to continue to hurt myself when there is another way? Can

I handle seemingly unpleasant situations in my life and still remain beautiful?

When I told Lilian this story, she asked, obviously amused, "I've been there. What if he hadn't given you the coffee you asked for, or if he hadn't apologized. Then what?"

I knew that she and I shared similar triggers in situations like this and I anticipated her question. "That would have been disappointing. At one point, I was prepared to just go and get my money back. But the victory for me is not about the outcome. We always concentrate on the outcome, on getting what we think we want. Your beauty isn't dependent on outcomes or expectations, which are always conditional."

"That's news."

"It's about the experience you want to have in the moment," I offered. "It's choosing not to abandon your beauty for any reason. That's where the practice lies. You want to be who you know you are through the entire process. For example, you want to be inspirational during your entire interaction. You don't want to have a single moment where you forget that. If the other person makes an ugly choice, that is on him, but you don't need to follow him there. You can still be on purpose, fully in your beauty. Why is there a need to become angry?"

Lilian frowned. "So even if he hadn't apologized, even if he hadn't changed the drink, you could still have had a 'care' victory? I don't know, Quinntin, Mother Teresa probably shouted at someone at least once for getting her coffee wrong. Nobody's that perfect at seven in the morning."

"It's not about perfection, but intention. I could have stayed in Care throughout the entire exchange. The care is more important than the outcome of my just getting what I want. Because remember, what do I really want? To be caring and to feel cared for because that is who I am. There has to have been a way for me to get the same result without going through my conditioning. If I was thinking about Care, my response would have been a caring response from the start. I might have said, 'If you're very concerned about this, I'd like to speak with your manager,' or 'I hear what you're saying, but this is what I need from you right now.' I went straight to anger. For someone else, that might be fine, but what I had to explore is that when I am in my condition, anger for me *is* the only choice. Acceptance means that I have to consider there may be another way.

"Remember that Beauty, my first word, is expressed through Care. And if the care I am looking for in that moment doesn't happen with him, it will happen somewhere else. But his behavior doesn't dictate whether I care or not and I don't give him the power to decide how I relate to my experience. That's the shift. That's a victory for me."

"Well, I never thought a story about coffee would help me deal with my sister…" Lilian said, laughing.

"By criticizing, judging, defending, we stay stuck. It's all learned behavior. Confronting people in fear, that's not a direction. That's not a purpose. That's a reaction. The direction is always to be true to self. But you have to trust yourself first.

"I shared that story with you to say this: your bringing inspiration to the world is bigger than who is right and who is wrong, or sibling rivalry, or parental approval. It's not about any of that at all. The message isn't about how to manipulate the other person so that I feel safe enough in any situation to be beautiful. The question is, why was I tempted or triggered to go back to my conditioning and forget my truth?"

"I think I understand," Lilian said. "What was happening with Marie on the phone was that my inspiration was up for negotiation. So, I have to ask myself, what is going on with me that my purpose can be abandoned so easily? I've chosen to step outside myself in order to fight, defend. But if I am in my condition to the point where I feel the need to protect myself, I don't need to change Marie, I need to find out what wound is triggering me to keep making that choice. It's not for me to convince her. I need to know what is causing me to lose my connection to self, and work from there."

"Exactly."

"I'll call Marie later tonight. But before I call, I'll concentrate on inspiration. I need to recognize what is truth for me and commit to that first." Lilian stood up and reached for her purse. She hugged me, and asked before leaving, "By the way, did you ever see the barista again?"

"I saw him the next day."

"I'm curious, if you don't mind, what did you say to him?"

"I concentrated on Care before I ordered. Actually, before I walked into the shop. Then I went up to the counter, he made my drink, and I said, 'Good Morning' and 'Thank you.' And he smiled and said, 'Good morning, Sir.' My drink was perfect. One of the best I've had. But even if he hadn't responded that way, I was clear that I was going to have a beautiful experience that morning, no matter what. Pride and my conditioning, of course, shouted, 'I'm not going to say good morning to him, are you kidding, after what he did to me?' But with acceptance, the voice of my purpose was stronger. I decided to care for myself in that moment, which automatically meant caring for him."

"Then what happened?"

"The rest of the day was beautiful."

Several weeks after our earlier conversation, I returned to Corrine's house for dinner. She greeted me warmly and I was impressed with how stunning she appeared, her hair casually swiped up and wearing what appeared to be a vintage de la Renta caftan. She had a cooking spoon in her hand, and, I was surprised to see, no phone. I hugged her and she invited me to sit on a barstool in a kitchen as she stirred something in a large pot that smelled delicious. After she put a glass of wine in my hand and turned down the stove to simmer, we moved to the sofa and she sat down beside me.

"I've put a lot of thought into what we talked about," she said. "The whole acceptance thing. I was skeptical at first, but I've been watching my conversations, just listening to myself. And I think you were right. I was complaining about my ex with a friend of mine just the other day and when I got off the phone, I felt inside like, 'I don't want to do this anymore. It's been years of the same conversation about him, over and over again. It's just not worth it!'

"Then something happened at work the other day. You know, the typical thing that just sends me right over the edge. I was getting angry, but I caught myself, and I thought about my purpose, Nourish, and what kind of experience I wanted to have in that moment. I asked myself, 'What do you really want?' I knew I didn't want to be angry. I had been having a really good day and this was one of those situations that I would later point to and say, 'Everything was fine until so-and-so ruined everything.' But this time, I decided I wasn't going to give this event that kind of power over me. I had to deal with what happened, of course, but I was committed to staying in my power. I thought, How can I bring my radiance to this moment? What does nourishing myself and others look like right now?

"I won't bore you with all the details," she continued, "but I could tell my co-worker was waiting for a huge confrontation. Instead of getting angry with her, I asked her what she needed. After I listened, I told her what I needed from her, that I would do my best to support her in the future and what I hoped would change. Then I handled the situation and let it go. I felt so much freer, and I think she was totally shocked. I kept thinking about what is true in this moment and what is my truth and what kind of day I want to have. And my truth always is, I want to be nourishing in my life as often as I can. I want anywhere I work to be a nourishing place. I want to be in charge of my happiness. Not anyone else."

Corrine took a large sip of wine and sighed. "Then my ex called again yesterday, and I have to say, I tried to be nourishing with him, but I just couldn't get there. I felt like crap. I know it is possible to have a different experience with him, and one day maybe I will, and I could see my conditioning taking over and I couldn't do anything about it. But I did consider for the first time that maybe nourishing myself is not speaking to him for a while. I didn't make the best choice in my conversation with him, but at least I know now there is a choice. And I've never felt that before. So, thank you for challenging me."

"Of course."

"Now," she said, standing up, and offering a hand. "I hope you're very hungry because that shrimp gumbo over there - a recipe from my great-grandmother – isn't going to eat itself!"

When we are afraid to be who we are, our conditioning becomes our truth. It's a sad fact that many of us live and make most of our decisions from our conditioning. The conditioning is so powerful that we "become" our condition – actors in the world but unwilling to live the truth of who we are. We know we are wearing a mask, but after a while it gets to be too much trouble to take it off. So, instead of challenging our thinking and acknowledging that we are in pain, we dress it up, adorn it, make it ours. But in the end, it is still a mask. This is what it means to live an unfulfilled life.

Our conditioning makes us feel separated from the world, isolated, constantly defensive. Beauty, on the other hand, is inclusive, everyone is invited. What we give to the world, we give to ourselves. You are the only one who can lead from truth: when you lead from truth, it is irresistible. We are all invited in that moment to feel beautiful. Nothing is more compelling than being in the presence of people who truly love themselves.

Our purpose is our truth. We are taught that beauty is conditional; that we have to wait for the right time, the right circumstances, or the right person before we can be fully in our beauty, before we can engage. But this is a limiting, destructive belief. Acceptance ultimately frees us, because it means that we let go of the need to manipulate and control until we realize that we already have what we want.

Acceptance is a process of surrendering in which we stop fighting to get approval, to gain acceptance from others. Our third word represents our purpose, what we have come to understand through the process of Trust, Discover, Describe and Visualize, guiding us to our beautiful experience. The situations in which we find ourselves reveal us to ourselves, as we consciously look at our lives, see what's true, and respond with truth. The fifth step, Accept, is the critical point of awareness; the moment when we understand that we can go into the world each day, radiating our beauty, and knowing – and this is the true meaning of acceptance – that whatever is happening in a given moment, whatever our circumstances, it doesn't define our ability to be beautiful. The world changes overnight when you change your mind about the world.

As you apply this chapter to your own life, observe the moments when you find you are triggered to go into a reactive place, into your negative conditioning. The conditioning will lead you to places of blame, defensiveness, and fear. If you are able to step back and see yourself in that moment, which is difficult for most people, try and make a different choice. Remember your purpose. If you are unsure or feel stuck, sometimes it is better to take a break from the experience until you are clear. Be patient with the learning process.

The process of acceptance is forever deepening. There is always more to learn about yourself. Choose to move into acceptance now.

Gandhi said, "Be the change you wish to see in the world." This is a beautiful statement of acceptance. Gandhi knew that the reality he faced and the oppression in that historical moment were true; but being oppressed wasn't his truth. His truth was the liberation that he conceived for himself and all of India. When you go into the world leading from purpose, you leave others no choice but to respond to your beauty. The moment you are no longer willing to negotiate your truth in the world, that's when you are ready to appear.

Appear

The sixth step, Appear, begins the moment you choose to exist.

The textbook definition of appear doesn't go far enough for our Truth of Beauty work together. When considering the potential for a beautiful life, the experience most of us call "existence" is too often defined by regret and compromise. We live in a world that may feel unsafe and harsh, and most of our time is spent avoiding or escaping from pain – with occasional moments of relief. We go from one interaction to another playing out familiar scripts based on our conditioned responses; our relationships are a series of negotiations to get what we want. We wait for someone else's behavior to change for us to have the experience we desire in the world. We blame the people in the past for why we feel stuck in the present. We withhold our true selves from the world out of fear, waiting for the day when someone will give us permission for our "real self" to appear.

This may sound a bit extreme, but for the majority of people I've worked with, it's really not too far off. There are, of course, birthdays and holidays and vacations and dinners with good friends. The pain of life is not unremitting, but it is often consistent. On a fundamental level, we live with the sense that there is something profoundly missing in our lives and we don't know what to do about it. Life, in fact, feels like something we have to get through, rather than living. I've spoken with many people who decided at some point that a beautiful life was unobtainable, and that being their true selves in the world was completely out of the question. For those of us who yearn for a deeply intimate expression of self, to be supported for who we are in the world, we may feel on some level that we don't exist at all. Just because you're being seen doesn't mean you are appearing.

Appear in the Truth of Beauty context means we reach the point where we are no longer willing to negotiate about showing up. We choose to be ourselves at all times in all situations. This may sound simple, and as a concept it is – it's the application that is challenging. When we show up in the world, fully living from our truth, it can bring up resistance in ourselves and others. The temptation is strong to return to the familiar, to go back into our closets of fear, where it feels "safe". In Truth of Beauty, existence isn't assumed; it takes work. Being fully in our purpose, regardless of what the world says or does in response, requires courage and stamina. For those for whom the world hasn't always felt like the safest place, learning to bring our truth into the world, not just when the "coast is clear" but 24/7, can at times be a terrifying experience.

When we assess the journey we've undertaken so far in the Truth of Beauty process, remember that we began with Trust. We had to ask the question, How do I get to my beauty, where do I start? We came to understand that we couldn't even approach our beauty without having a firm trust in ourselves. With a memory of trust to guide us, Discovery meant taking that trust to the next level, and asking, "What is it that I need to know, who am I and what matters most to me?"

Once we understood the power of our third word in our lives, and its role in defining our purpose in Describe, we began to express ourselves consciously.

Through Visualize we began to envision the possibility of a life in which we were in our truth more than we were ruled by our conditioning.

When we reached the stage of Accept, we realized that if we were ever going to be truly ourselves, we'd have to be honest about our reality. Accept helped us understand that if we wanted lasting change, we could no longer blame "them" for our choices or experiences; we'd have to begin with an examination of self. We began to realize that to move forward and be who we are, we would have to accept all that is in our lives – past and present – without denial. No more games, no more lies or cover-ups. Only by facing the truth could we change the focus of the conversation back to where it belonged: our relationship to ourselves.

Appear is a natural progression from the step of Accept. Some of the people I have worked with have overcome extraordinary difficulties to reach this stage. There is nothing more beautiful than the decision as adults to appear, when too often what has been affirmed in childhood is someone else's desire that we should disappear.

As a child, I was told repeatedly that the way I was being treated would one day make me stronger and that I would be grateful, that the abusive patterns I'd been taught would toughen me up. What I learned instead was to look out into the world with an expectation of the same type of abuse. I drew this energy to me and created abusive experiences from which I had to protect myself even though abuse was the last thing I wanted. What I really wanted was care.

Acceptance never means agreeing that abusive behavior is okay. It means understanding that in order to heal, we have to realize that changing our lives doesn't require us to control or change someone else. The irony of acceptance is that until we are able to accept, we cannot let go. Accept is critical to Appear; it allows us to release our history and move on. We may not have all the answers at first, but the moment we are willing to consider there may be another way to exist outside of the pain of our condition, we begin to appear.

Appear is purposely sequenced as one of Truth of Beauty's final steps because it signifies a psychological point of no return. At this juncture, I tell my clients, "You've seen too much to go back to a life solely defined by your conditioning. You are aware now that you are responsible for your beautiful experience, that you always were from the beginning." Living in the world and making choices based on truth rather than our conditioning can feel deeply uncomfortable, while at the same time familiar, like meeting an old friend.

Just because you're being seen doesn't mean you are appearing.

It may return us all the way back to the beginning of the process, to our first experience of trusting ourselves and loving ourselves unconditionally. We are in Trust again, only this time not as children, but as conscious adults. Appear marks a homecoming, a beautiful return to self.

Appear is an action step, requiring us to test ourselves against the outside world. We've lived in the "real world" from birth and felt forced to adjust to its perceptions. Conditioning has taught us to learn to be who the outside world tells us we are. We reinforce this conditioning over the years as a means of protection, a temporary defense, with the hope that one day, if we are lucky, we will be able to reveal our true selves without compromise. Years pass, and we discover that the conditioning we have learned and empowered through fear and habit has now become what is true for us in the world. It is, of course, not our actual truth, but what supplants the truth. This is the point where many people give up, deciding it is easier to maintain a façade than admit they are in pain. Appear opens us up to a new world.

The majority of the Truth of Beauty work we have done up to this point has been internal – we have questioned ourselves at the deepest levels and visualized how we want to be in the world.

When we appear, we take that deeper understanding and apply it to our everyday experiences. Appear is literally beauty in action. Until you choose to appear, beauty, as we've defined it, is theoretical; a set of ideas and guidelines. Appear is where beauty manifests as a daily spiritual practice and commitment. Whether we choose to go fast or slow is not important, what defines our experience is our commitment to living our truth. When we find ourselves in situations we don't like, we don't choose fear and abandon our purpose, and we don't blame someone else. We go deeper into purpose and allow it to continue to illuminate our path.

There is a pleasure you can feel only when you show up in the world as you never have before. It is where you take your place in the world as a true individual, with the knowledge that whatever the world presents to you, you can respond with truth rather than fear or aggression. When people meet you, they are no longer seeing an identity motivated by a reaction to negative conditioning, but the person you know yourself to be. Mere existence in its crudest definition is another way of saying "taking up space." In contrast, living your truth in the world is power, and the essence of beauty.

Julia, a client of mine who works in finance, walked into work one morning to discover her boss had been fired. Days later, she was told that someone new was being brought into the office to take her boss'

place. When the new boss, Adam, showed up, a transfer from another office, he was preceded by a reputation for getting results fast, and also for being difficult, demanding and something of a dictator. Having grown up with an alcoholic father who often bullied her, Julia immediately felt anxiety about this man's arrival.

Julia soon discovered that she would report directly to Adam and have to work closely with him on several projects. She was also aware that even though Adam had only been there a short time, a co-worker had already left a staff meeting in tears, and one of his assistants had threatened to quit.

Having reached the step of Appear in our Truth of Beauty work, Julia knew that she couldn't do what her conditioning was already telling her to do: get into bed and hide under the covers; use up all her sick leave; and escape. She had to remain in her truth. What Adam thought didn't matter: if she truly wanted to appear, negotiation with anyone else would be futile and misdirected. Her goal was to remember her purpose and her third word, Affirm, no matter what Adam said, or thought, or did.

In our sessions, Julia and I discussed her relationship with her father. She had come to a place of acceptance in that relationship. She'd faced some unpleasant memories about her childhood and how those experiences contributed to her conditioning. Because of that courageous, honest work, Julia didn't have to go into this work situation projecting her experience with her father onto Adam. Her father was her father, and Adam was a man for whom she worked. She accepted her family history and decided, by bringing it into consciousness and not running from it, to let it go. That part of her story felt very clean and clear.

On the morning she was to meet Adam in his office to start their first project together, she knew exactly what her conditioning wanted her to do, but she didn't block it out. She listened and acknowledged her fear and the familiar insecurities. She then made a choice; she got dressed in her favorite suit, treated herself to a relaxed breakfast, and went to work, walking into the office on time and with confidence. And she decided that her commitment to her truth, even when it felt scary, meant more to her life than choosing the familiar "safe" patterns of her conditioning. What was true was that she felt afraid of Adam and she was going to work anyway. She decided, in that moment, to appear.

Julia observed over the course of several weeks that a relationship with Adam could exist without fear or animosity. She could see that Adam took up a lot of space in the minds of the people who disliked him, and she didn't want that burden – she'd lost too many years to that energy by resenting and not accepting her relationship with her father. Her main concern in her working relationship with Adam was how to stay in her truth – "How do I continue to appear as I really am, as my true self?"

Julia continued to remember her third word, Affirm, and what it meant to her. She was known for her positive approach to situations, and she had a reputation in the office for making people feel better and supporting them with positivity. She soon discovered that even when Adam was in a foul mood with others he still relied on her, because of her ability to give her co-workers confidence and clear instruction, all part of her ability to affirm.

A day came when Adam shouted for her to come into his office; a team member had made a mistake and he was furious. Adam needed to vent at someone, and she was nearby. He shut the door but his anger was audible from outside, as she knew from one of his tantrums weeks before. The diatribe definitely triggered her and reminded her of her past, but she grounded herself, allowed him to finish, and again asked herself, How do I want to respond in this moment – from my conditioning or from truth? How do I want to visualize myself in this situation and how do I appear – not to Adam, or my co-workers, but to myself?

Julia again chose to go deeper into her third word, Affirm. The word felt very close, very personal. She let her purpose word lead her and found that what she needed most was to affirm herself in her response to Adam. In processing the experience with Julia, I acknowledged that times like these were the most challenging and rewarding because technically she had every excuse in the world to respond from a feeling of victimization. Instead, commitment to her third word meant that Julia took a powerful action. In her loyalty to her purpose, Affirm, we could see that her second or aspirational word, Decisiveness, led us back to her foundation word, Community – what she wanted to create in the world. For Julia, having a work environment that felt like a community was essential to fulfilling her purpose. She felt Adam's toxic behavior disrupted her sense of community in her workspace. She knew in this moment that decisiveness was called for.

"I've enjoyed working together on this project, Adam," she began, "and I hope that we can continue to work together in the future." She observed his face, which was now red, and the way he gripped the chair with both hands, but she knew from his penetrating stare that she had his attention.

"But I must insist that you never to speak to me in that tone of voice again. I consider that abusive behavior, and I won't work with you under those conditions for any reason. I'm leaving now."

She walked from his office to the elevator as the others watched, and returned to the office hours later when she felt ready. Julia's story didn't end with Adam "seeing the light" and becoming a new person because of their confrontation. He did, however, apologize and remained respectful towards her in their working relationship. Julia also took steps when necessary to protect others from Adam's toxic behavior based on her desire to protect the community.

Julia remarked in our follow-up session on how powerful she felt, and her awareness that the words she said to Adam she had never been able to say to her father. As a child, she'd often felt trapped by her father's behavior, but even as an adult woman, she'd never felt she could just walk out of the room and tell her father no. Appearing with Adam changed all of that.

Julia could recall a time in her life when her initial response would have been to call every friend she had, to complain, to ask what she should do, and then engage in passive-aggressive ways to sabotage her work on the project because she didn't feel safe confronting Adam directly or telling him what she needed. Her decision to appear meant that she didn't need to engage in shadow power to get what she needed anymore.

"I'm not saying I'm grateful that Adam yelled at me," she said, "I'm not. But I will say this: it felt good to tell him my truth. And when I left the office, I felt like I was floating. Like I'd just run a marathon. I didn't know that an ugly situation like that could be transformed into something beautiful, simply because I chose to appear."

As you may recall, an essential part of the Truth of Beauty process is going into our history to appreciate where our early conditioning comes from. We use this information as a point of reference; further along in the process we find out we must accept this story and be willing to release our attachment to it in order for us to Appear.

A client of mine, Greg, also struggled with his ability to appear. In fact, with his life-long feelings of inadequacy and self-loathing, and the messages he heard growing up, he was actively trying to disappear. Greg was in his late thirties and had come from a wealthy family; he'd had success in his education and business, and knew how to exude sophistication and class in all the right situations. But speaking with him intimately, I often felt as if I were talking to a little boy. Whenever it seemed we were making progress, Greg brought the conversation back to his parents, his childhood, and what he felt was denied him growing up. He seemed to return to his past in every example he gave. He could recount what happened fifteen years ago with great detail, but his memory of what happened yesterday was a bit fuzzy. Every story, no matter how contemporary, returned to his early beginnings and the disappointment he felt. He couldn't get past several key experiences which he defined as ultimate betrayals. It was as if his life were on hold, waiting for a moment when justice or even revenge would one day make him whole.

Greg collected memorabilia of famous actors from the Forties and Fifties and knew everything about the Golden Age of Television and Hollywood during the studio era. He could talk about Bette Davis and Joan Crawford and Jack Warner for hours. When I brought up the subject of his own dreams of being an actor, a goal that his family hadn't encouraged, he shut down and quickly changed the subject. Despite the pain the childhood memories brought him, I observed that he was fully animated only when he recalled the past or the fantasy world of Hollywood. When I visited his home, I saw the rows of papers and magazines in tall stacks, photos that lined the walls, and I knew he was proud of everything he had collected. At the same time, I was also aware that he had created a fortress in his apartment, a way to protect himself from his fear of the world. After I left, I considered what it would take for this man to appear in his life.

Greg had come to me because he said that he wanted to break free, he wanted to be released, and I believed him. But I knew we couldn't move into Appear until he was able to accept his past and the truth about his choices. I needed him to fall out of love with his history and his limitations, which is one example of what it means to decide to appear. Until Greg could acknowledge that what had happened to him was not the raison d'être but the departure point for our work together, appearing for him was impossible.

Greg isn't alone. Given my profession, I've met people from all walks of life, people with money and fame, who have made great achievements in their careers and who have earned widespread admiration. If you see them in the public eye or in magazines you will probably believe otherwise, but many of them are just not happy. Greg had all the privilege and the advantages that most people assume automatically lead to success. He was surprised when I told him there was nothing more I could offer him until he was willing to risk envisioning a life in which his conditioning no longer had authority over him.

I share Greg's story because there are times when, as much as we may feel pain from our conditioning and the role it plays in our lives, it can be very comfortable. If we are unable to acknowledge that our belief system has negative power over us, then we cannot appear. When we refuse to release our history, like Greg, it is often because we feel the opposite of what it means to Appear, which is shame. Shame encourages us to hide from the world, to keep pretending that even though we are miserable, nothing is wrong. Over the years we add layer after layer of denial. We move from one shame-inducing experience to another, like a moving target, so that we cannot be seen or touched by anyone. Shame is devastating to our beautiful experience. The unfortunate thing is that often the behavior we feel ashamed about isn't even ours. I've worked with people who carry family shame around the way the moon eclipses the sun, blocking their light from being seen in the world. We can't appear when we are stuck in chronic shame or when we are apologizing for who we are. We have to risk challenging the assumption of shame, no matter how long we've lived with that pattern, in order to experience what it means to appear. Our ability to live fully in truth may not happen all at once, we may have setbacks, but once we reach the sixth step we acknowledge that no matter what we feel about who we are, we can no longer hide – behind our history, behind other people, behind our fear. We appear! And when faced with our conditioning, we resist the temptation to disappear.

I spoke with Lilian several times before her mother's birthday celebration and she kept me updated on her relationship with her sister Marie. There had definitely been an improvement, she said, and for the first time from as far back as she could remember Lilian felt that Marie was actually listening and taking her seriously. It was a transformational moment for their relationship. Sometimes there were temporary challenges when old patterns emerged, but Lilian continued to stay the course, determined to appear to her sister and to her family. They saw her authority and acknowledged her leadership in subtle ways. Something indeed was shifting. I commended her for her commitment to herself; all of this was possible because she had accepted the truth about her relationship with her sister, and she agreed.

As Lilian and her sister continued to work together without resentment, Lilian considered the possibility that she and Marie might one day be as close as friends. Her decision to appear had moved her into vulnerability, able to acknowledge for the first time the profound sadness underneath all their fighting, and the fact that she had missed having a loving sister in her life. Getting in touch with this pain meant Lilian responded differently to Marie, that her tone was gentler, less defensive. The more Lilian appeared, the less she felt she had to fight to get what she needed. The reward was a new relationship with herself first, and vulnerability with Marie, a feeling she had lost since they were children.

Appear, perhaps the most critical turning-point in our Truth of Beauty process, requires great faith. For clients who have serious trust issues or damage from their religious backgrounds, just hearing the word faith can bring up defensiveness. But there is no other word. Once Appear lays our foundation, there is a jumping-off point to destinations and experiences unknown. We know we can't return to our conditioning, which is familiar, and we haven't developed the strength to be fully in the world yet. We have to rely on something during our transition while we experiment with what it means to appear. The faith we require is faith in ourselves.

Appear requires us to be fully in present time –
we cannot refer to our history as a guide for what will
happen to us today when we are appearing. To appear
means to meet each beautiful moment with a sense of
discovery. The energy of appear may feel childlike, playful,
and new. We are affirming to the world, "I'm here!" It may
also feel terrifying, a real sense of letting go. Some of
us may not remember the last time we felt we really
appeared. Possibly, we may have to go all the way back
to the examples we gave when we were working on
Trust. We may feel joy, delight, anger, sadness, grief and
adventure – all at the same time!

When appearing feels too dangerous, we may
choose to respond to life from safety and what is
familiar. Life becomes rehearsed and stale like the
actor who keeps performing the same role for years in
different cities and can't find a new interpretation. We
may go through the motions of change but never break
through. The isolation is total, because no one sees the
real us, not even ourselves. It is a sad bargain, holding
onto our condition because it is what we know, while
giving up the potential for an authentic, loving and
honest relationship with another human being. It is
possible not to be narcissistic and still fall in love with
yourself, with your life. Our love of self is essential to
our ability to love others.

We have to challenge ourselves to be ourselves. We have to appreciate where the pain comes from when we choose to appear, and then move on without judgement. Like a tiny campfire in the woods which we build and blow on gently to keep lit, and which we feed so that it warms us through the night, we have to nurture ourselves through Appear. In Appear, we win, not by others' reaction to us, but because of our intention to keep showing up, even when we don't immediately see the results we want, or when we feel insecurity or pain. As I offered to one client, "Of course you feel pain: every time you tried to be yourself in the past, you were told, No. You developed a personality, a condition to protect yourself, to respond to no. The question now is: Who are you when the answer is yes?"

Appear returns us to our second, or aspirational word. You may recall from the chapter Discover that our second word is a quality we feel we were lacking and that is required in order to achieve our purpose. I chose the word Strength. Strength is what I felt I needed in order to bring beauty into the world through my third word of Care. As I shared earlier, I grew up feeling weak in myself and had been told that I was weak (even though I often suspected deep down from an early age that I was strong). Part of the problem was that whenever I showed strength, my guardians saw my strength as disobedience and I was punished. I formed a personality around the belief that I wasn't strong and convinced myself in later years that strength was something that I needed to attain. I couldn't appreciate that strength wasn't something new and foreign to me, but was something that, as a result of my early conditioning and because of fear, I had simply misplaced. When I chose to appear, I went deeper into Care, my third word, and discovered I had more opportunities to follow my purpose, to care for others and know that I had everything I needed. I was strong, because care, when practiced with conviction, is strong – strength in action.

The exercise we used for locating your second word was essential earlier in the process because it revealed to us what we felt we needed in order to appear. When we choose to appear, our second word immediately manifests in our lives. In the sixth step, we don't need to separate our second word any longer – it will always appear when we are fully committed to our first and third word. The second word is a quality we've always had, inherent in our foundation word and obscured by our conditioning, just waiting to come out. It has only been our perception that it is something we aspire to. But the fact that we choose it reveals that it is as essentially ours as our foundation and purpose words.

Identifying our second word was critical to the challenge of appearing. We needed to know where we believed our weakness was to appreciate what was behind the conditioning. When you return to your second word after reading this chapter, consider the quality you chose at that time and ask yourself: has it truly been missing from my life, or waiting for me to appear and claim it? Like the beautiful Lion in *The Wizard of Oz,* who never needed the wizard to give him courage but could not have reached that understanding without the journey of facing his greatest fear, your second word is part of that same heroic journey.

While we may return to our second word from time to time as a reminder of a quality that we value, the fact remains: there is no lack and nothing to achieve. You have everything you need to appear from purpose. You always have.

Scott came by for a session one weekend. He was starting a romantic relationship and had just gotten promoted at work. He was more creative than ever before. He felt he had great success during Visualize but, given the resentment he still harbored about family, the stage of Accept had been much harder. Now, Appear was proving to be his Waterloo, near impossible – he felt like he had crashed against solid rock. He expressed his frustration almost as soon as he walked in the door.

"I'm afraid," he said, "that if I am fully me, one hundred percent, all of me, someone is going to leap out and say, 'To hell with you, man' and drive me right back underground. And I want to be vulnerable in this new relationship. I want my partner to really see me." He told me that he felt himself wanting to go into falseness because it was a familiar pattern – vulnerability was still too new. With that line of thinking, if she rejected his mask, he could always save face knowing that he had kept something in reserve, something she hadn't had access to. I offered, "Then you get to say to yourself, 'She didn't really reject me because she never got the real me in the first place.'"

Whether we are hiding inside ourselves or somewhere out in the world, hiding is all about shame, and we can't live a shame-based life and appear. At some point, Scott was going to have to reveal more of himself.

He looked miserable. "But what if she decides to break up with me because she doesn't like what she sees?"

"It's not about her," I reminded him. "Acceptance means that you have to accept the fact that she is going to think whatever she wants about you and you have no control over that whatsoever.

"When you used to hide behind a mask in your other relationships, you felt you were in control, because you could put your mask on and take it off whenever you felt like it; but that was an illusion. You're not in control now any more than you were then."

"You're right, I'm not."

"We think we are safe behind the mask, but in some ways that's the most dangerous place to be. Appearing, while scarier, is actually the safest place. Because it is all of you, living your purpose. There's no compartmentalization, no guesswork, no way to fall through the cracks. When you sit down to dinner and talk, you'll know she's really seeing who you are."

"I know! That's what scares the hell out of me. I haven't let anybody see that Scott in a while, definitely not in a new relationship. I don't care if she rejects the other Scott, the fake guy who doesn't trust anyone. But the real Scott? That's too painful."

"There's only one Scott when you choose to appear. You have a chance to decide to be vulnerable because it's the experience that you want to have in this world. Let's leave her aside for now. Remember: just go deeper into Compassion. Let compassion guide you through this. You can't go deeper into your third word and remain locked in this much fear. It's impossible.

"You want this to be a transformative experience for both of you, because that's your foundation. As you go deeper into transformation, you'll find the audacity from the second word – the courage you need – is waiting for you. Whenever you've trusted yourself in a situation of transformation, you've always been bold. Remember, you're sharing your compassionate experience with her, you're not waiting for her to bring it to you. Stay in your purpose."

"I feel like an idiot for being nervous, but a lot of this feels new. I like her, I want this to be right."

"Make the decision that you want to appear, that you want to take the chance of really being seen. If for some reason she doesn't agree with what she sees, it will be okay. You're showing up for yourself, that's what matters. It may be tomorrow, it may be a week or a month from now, but someone will see your truth and fall in love with it. But they can only find you when you appear – not for anyone else, but for yourself."

Melissa, a woman in her mid-forties, came to me on the advice of her friend for a beauty consultation. Five minutes in, we ended up discussing her frustration with her wife Stacey. Melissa has struggled with compulsive eating and body-image issues most of her life. In our first session together, she recounted memories from her childhood which she still found painful, of having been teased by her whole family at one time or another about her weight. Sometimes her four brothers and sister were the worst offenders, and she felt her parents rarely protected her from their cruelty.

"I watched my brothers, who were rail-thin and athletic, eat whatever they wanted, while I was encouraged to go on diets as early as the age of six," she explained to me. She described one evening when her father's co-worker and his wife were visiting for dinner. In front of everyone, her mother asked if she thought having a second helping of mashed potatoes "was a good idea," and took the serving spoon out of her hand after everyone else had helped themselves. Melissa was twelve. She made an excuse about homework and a paper due the next day and left the table in tears.

Melissa was embarrassed by the incident but apologized to me, suggesting it was a "small thing in the past which shouldn't even matter anymore". I reassured her that the story was important to identifying her conditioning and to arriving at what she needed to accept. Without acceptance, on some level, more than thirty years later and 2,000 miles away from her family of origin, she was still twelve, still humiliated at that table.

Melissa continued to diet through her twenties and thirties, feeling the same pressure that she had as a child – this time from herself. She acknowledged that eventually the frustration and deprivation from the dieting would become so great that she would overeat and experience the familiar feelings of despair. When she met Stacey, her partner of twelve years and now wife, she was determined to change her behavior for good so that it wouldn't define their relationship. Stacey, who had never known the pain of an eating disorder and had grown up in a mostly supportive family, often tried to "help" Melissa by suggesting exercise programs, healthy food, getting enough sleep. There were articles shared from online magazines and links to healthy cooking websites. Melissa tried to appreciate the support but most of the time she just felt enraged.

"I know she means well," Melissa sighed. "And it's partly my fault. I make declarations that I'm not going to eat as much sugar or that I'm giving up fast food forever, and then two days later she finds candy bars in the cupboards or a fast food receipt, and she can't help but be disappointed with me. The other day, she found some snack food I'd sworn off, potato chips or something, and she held it up, sighed, and reminded me that I said I wanted to stop eating so much junk."

I asked her how she felt in that moment. "I felt like I was seven, being shamed by my mother because I wanted to eat my Halloween candy like my brothers and sisters only she threw most of mine away. Or the way I felt when I had to shop in the section of the store with bigger sizes."

Her face showed obvious pain at the memory. "Stacey and I have a wonderful relationship; I love her and I know she means well. But in those moments, I can't help it, I just attack, and I start shouting at her to stop putting so much pressure on me. I feel cornered and overwhelmed. Then she gets upset and probably confused because she doesn't know how to support me when what I tell her I want changes from one day to the next."

Melissa had originally come to talk about a "makeover" but our conversation had gone to places much deeper. She seemed a little reluctant at first to go into the painful childhood memories and her current situation, but later honestly admitted that even if we talked about hair length and her fall colors, she wouldn't be able to take it in for long because of her body dysmorphia and self-hate.

I could see from my initial meeting with Melissa that she took great pride in her appearance – from her polished nails and carefully styled blonde hair, to the attention with which she selected her clothes and her expensive perfume. Every time she walked through the door looking fabulous, she apologized immediately for the way she looked. She later told me that female friends of hers, especially women at work, were always complimenting her style and saying how beautiful she was, even when she was at her heaviest. One friend asked if Melissa would shop with her and help her develop a style. Despite all the loving attention, she still felt empty.

"I have problems seeing myself," she admitted. "I always have. I take a lot of care to look nice, and then when people compliment me, I feel numb, as if they are talking about someone else. I would like to be more powerful in my life, but I feel stuck. And I'm exhausted arguing with Stacey. I married her because I wanted a life partner, not a personal trainer. I feel like we've both put her in that role, but I don't know how to stop it."

Melissa and I worked together for some time before we were able to shift the focus off her frustration with Stacey and her weight issues, back onto her third word, Kindness. Her first word was Stability, her second word, Courage. Kindness was what she was looking for from her partnership, it defined her interactions with the young children she cared for, the animals she'd rescued, and her overall vision of the world. Stability was important to Melissa's life, and in all her interactions she created that stability through acts of kindness. She found herself willing to extend kindness to all people, it seemed, but herself. When she approached her romantic relationship expecting kindness, she experienced Stacey acting like her mother – controlling and critical. Courage, her aspirational word, was what she felt she needed to speak up for herself.

Often she was just silent, as she had been in childhood, too ashamed to defend herself. As a result, over the course of their marriage, they had variations on the same conflict, played out over and over again.

When Melissa and I spoke, she told me the latest of Stacey's transgressions. The stories varied slightly, but all roads led to the same place: why wouldn't Stacey stop pressuring her and change?

In one heated session, Melissa was exasperated because Stacey had bought her a local gym membership as a birthday gift. She was furious; she felt that Stacey was trying to shame her again. As she continued to go on about Stacey's presumption and thoughtlessness, I finally interrupted her.

"Melissa, I'd like you to take Stacey out of the conversation, and let's focus on you for a moment."

"Sure." She looked slightly surprised at the interruption, as if she hadn't been listening to herself.

"You are looking for Stacey to change, but we know that we can't change her. We can only work on you. Because, if we're honest, and move into a place of acceptance, you realize this negative talk and judgement didn't originate with Stacey, right?"

"Yes, that's true. It goes all the way back to my mother and her judgmental behavior. That's why it is so painful for me."

"So just as an exercise, I'd like to consider something. Instead of talking about Stacey or your mother, let's talk about you. Imagine that Stacey is just mirroring back to you some of your own self-talk.

She is just a mouthpiece for a belief system, or rather, she provides the words and experiences for a feeling that you are familiar with. It's almost like playing an old-fashioned jukebox. You put the quarter in, but the machine doesn't choose the song, you do."

"I see where this is going," Melissa said. "But I don't agree if you are saying that it's all my fault."

"It's not about fault," I said carefully. "It's about a feeling. And the attachment to that feeling, because even though it is hurtful and painful, it is familiar. And by staying in that feeling, it is difficult to accept the situation and fully appear."

"The feeling I always have is self-hatred and shame," she admitted. "I've known that most of my life."

"That's right. And we want to release that feeling, so we can experience another feeling, one that supports you. None of this is your fault, but it is your responsibility now that you've got it. Accept that it is there, wherever it came from, and decide it doesn't serve you any longer. Because we both know, what usually happens is that we say to someone, 'I hate this, stop giving me this feeling, I'm getting out of here,' and then we run around the corner and find someone else who gives us the same feeling. Stacey is responsible for her behavior, but we both know that she came late to this party, she is not where this originates in your life. And when the time is right, she'll take her cue – from you, Melissa. The question you need to ask yourself is: why am I still holding on to this feeling? What is the payoff for maintaining it and is it worth staying in that feeling at the cost of my beautiful life?"

"I've never felt beautiful," she cried openly. "Never. I think part of me feels like no matter what I do or think, it won't matter."

"You are beautiful," I told her. "And that's not just because people tell you that, even though that is true. You are beautiful because we are all inherently beautiful. But sometimes we have to work a little harder to bring it into our consciousness and get our negative conditioning out of the way. We have to face the fear. But nothing can begin until we move into a place of acceptance."

"What does acceptance look like?"

"I was going to ask you that question."

"Maybe it means realizing that I will never be able to please my mother or anyone else. I have to start with me. And that fighting with Stacey won't change the feeling I have about myself. Nor will trying to get her to change. It's not about her. As long as I make it about her, I don't have to change. And that's very safe. And if I'm angry, I give myself permission to eat. I'm attached to staying stuck because that is what feels familiar, that's home."

"Exactly." She reached for a tissue, and I gave her a moment before I said, "Go deeper into your third word, Melissa. Kindness. That's the feeling and expression that is missing in everything you've described. And yet I sense that it is what defines you in your relationship to everyone else and how most people see you. Get into that word, understand what it truly means. Don't assume you know. Let it guide you in the next couple of days. And be gentle with yourself. This is very powerful work you are doing. The feelings you are avoiding have a lot to say to you. It may feel like an enemy now, but it is the path that will lead you to acceptance. Only then can you appear."

Several weeks after our session, Melissa called me. Before she explained what had happened, I could already hear the excitement in her voice.

"I can't believe it," she said. "Something changed with me and Stacey already and I'm sort of in shock right now."

"I can't wait to hear."

"I told her that I was going to go for a week without soda and sugar drinks and of course, the very next day she found a bottle of soda in the refrigerator when she came home from work. I meant to drink it the night before or pour it out, and I had completely forgotten and left it in there. Although I'm starting to consider that maybe I did it on purpose, continuing this same old familiar cycle: I fail, she tries to help, I feel shamed by her and go quiet, she gets frustrated and leaves the room, seeing herself as the victim until we both apologize – our familiar dance.

"Anyway, she takes the soda out, and I hear the usual sigh. Then she gives me a look of concern, reminding me that my blood sugar was high at my last check-up and that I said only yesterday that I wanted to stop eating so much sugar. I felt for a moment the old anger, but this time I waited until she was finished, and I thought, 'What would kindness look like in this moment?' Not just towards her, but also towards myself and our relationship. She stood there waiting, the way my mother would stand there, wanting an explanation when she caught me eating something that wasn't on my diet. But this time, I was amazed by what came out of my mouth.

"I said, 'Stacey, I know you are giving me this feedback because you want me to be healthier and I want to say thank you because I also know it is coming from a place of love and you aren't judging me. And as soon as I am ready and feel strong enough to make a different choice, I will. But for now, I just want to say thank you and I love you. Thank you for caring about me.' Then I held her. "

"That's amazing."

"At first, I thought to myself, am I being sarcastic, is there a little bit of anger underneath what I'm saying… a 'go to hell' underneath? I know I can be passive-aggressive like that. But I truly didn't feel that at all. I felt at peace. I decided to let kindness lead me and I just started talking and that's what came out. And it was amazing because we've had so many fights where we've gone back and forth, and I've shut down believing I was being honest with her. I never felt better because I knew that in a week or two we'd be in the exact same place again. That energy feels so thick and negative between us, like choking on smog.

"But this felt lighter, like opening a window for fresh air. Almost effortlessly. It was incredible, the look on Stacey's face. She just stood there, like she was seeing me for the first time. And the strange thing is, in that moment, I felt like I saw her, too – and that she wasn't trying to control me or hurt me, she was genuinely worried that if I didn't take care of myself, she might find herself one day without me, alone. I let myself feel the sadness that I was harming myself and the powerlessness she felt over my choices. And I remembered that she'd taken care of her sick mother when she was a teenager, and her Mom died of cancer before Stacey graduated from high school. I knew that, but I hadn't really opened myself up to the pain she felt. It was all there, it has always been there, but I couldn't see or relate to any of it because everything had been filtered through my story. My need to fight back was so strong, all I could see from Stacey was judgement.

"Later that evening, I thought about my mother, how hard it has been for me to forgive her after all these years. I'm not saying I agree with every choice she made, but I also saw that she was concerned about me and did what she thought would help me. I considered saying the same words to her when I see her during the holidays. I thought, I can say this speech to her without anger because I truly feel it. Not just a bunch of words I usually throw at her to keep the peace. But truly from my heart. I feel freer."

I congratulated Melissa and we laughed together. A few moments later the energy shifted, and she was silent. She then shared with me her concern that the old conditioning would eventually come back, that it was just a brief moment of freedom, like a passing cloud, and that she would wake up and everything, the old judgments and fear, would be back again and things would return to "normal."

I reminded her, "What you felt with Stacey, when you spoke from your truth, that is normal. Not what you've been living until now. It is abnormal to live our lives separated from our truth. But that's not usually what the world tells us. You experienced in that moment what kindness and standing in your truth feel like. From what I'm hearing, you felt aligned. You felt powerful. You gave your relationship stability. And it wasn't about how much you weighed, or the soda in the fridge, or Stacey, or getting your mother's approval or anything external that needed to change for you to have that experience. The externals will change based on your internal work. You went deeper into your third word, and Kindness brought you to a place of understanding and vulnerability."

"It feels wonderful. But I don't want to just visit that town, as you've said, I want to live there. This is who I want to be all the time."

"This is who you are. And you can choose to appear and never look back. Even if you decide tomorrow to go back to the old way of thinking, you still can't 'un-know' this new feeling. Now you can appreciate, on the deepest level, the difference between your truth and conditioning. And you'll know immediately when you are in your conditioning, because it won't feel as good as this."

"I hope so," she said. "I'm tired of being in pain."

"This is what it means to appear," I said. "And it may take some practice at first. Don't give up. You said it seemed that Stacey was seeing you for the first time. In some ways, perhaps she is. She's never seen you show that much kindness towards yourself – not for her, for yourself. What you have now is an invitation, to perceive your life differently, to change the conversation to one that is based on who you really are, and not what you have been reacting to all these years. Every day we're making choices. And the conditioning is there whenever you want to pick it up, to help you blame, judge, defend or talk about what the other person isn't doing or giving that keeps you stuck. There are always people who will support that conversation, who will shake their heads and agree with you about how bad things are. It takes faith, once you have decided to appear, not to return to old defenses and patterns."

Like Melissa, you must trust that what is emerging is you. The real you. Trust that those who can appreciate the real you will want to come closer, will want to know more and support you, and those who are threatened will fall away. When you are in your truth, there is no deprivation – your love for yourself will always be enough. There may be some people for whom our truth is too much. We just stay committed to purpose in those moments. Your life will adjust to give you the beautiful experiences you desire.

Being our authentic selves doesn't happen automatically; it is a learning process. We've lived in the world on the world's terms, and we know how to experience life through the lens of our conditioning. Being our true selves and being in the world at the same time, as you've seen from the examples provided, can feel strange and new. It is one of the biggest assumptions, and leads to a great deal of shame, that we should just automatically know how to be ourselves. Living from truth in the world is a complicated dance and we need to be patient with ourselves, and with others.

We use the world as a sounding-board, a workshop, to help us identify where we are, what we are projecting. In our conditioning, we are looking for the world to tell us who we are. When we appear, *we* tell the world who we are. The world never validates you, it confirms you. If you are not seeing yourself in the world as you would like, the answer isn't to go out and stomp your feet or manipulate the world into getting what you want. Go back and learn more about you, go deeper into your purpose. When you are ready to appear, the world will see you. It has no other choice.

It is my hope as you continue this work that you become less attached to your history and more able to move into present time. There is a lot at stake. If you deny yourself your gift, you deny the world your gift, you deny it your purpose, and you deny your love. You also deny your happiness – the joy that inspires others.

So, practice, show up, go out of your way to present yourself, grow more into yourself. You are deciding each day how you want to live. You want to live in beauty, that's why you are here. If you hesitate, ask yourself, what am I waiting for? Sometimes the tiny steps are really the big steps. We feel the need to make big declarations, but in the end, it is your quiet power that announces real change. Stand in your truth and appear. Begin now and reveal all that is your beautiful self.

Own

What you own belongs to you.

We usually think of owning strictly in material terms. When you have paid for or financed something, there is a feeling of satisfaction. You can say with pride, I own the house I live in, this is my new car. We look in our closets and on our shelves and admire all the things we own. But what does it mean to take ownership of your life?

With the Sixth step of Appear, we stopped negotiating with others how we show up in the world. In the Seventh step, Own, we take the step that leads to lasting change – we stop negotiating with ourselves. It is our deepest confrontation with self that illuminates our path to beauty. When we decide no longer to negotiate our truth from within, we begin to understand, perhaps for the first time, what it means to take full ownership of who we are meant to be.

In order to ask the question, "Have I taken ownership of my life?" we must examine what a borrowed life looks like. A borrowed or rented life is a life that may appear to be yours, but can be taken back at any time by your conditioning or someone else's demands or expectations. Your power can still be given away in a moment. When we live borrowed lives, we exist in constant frustration, triggered by others' behavior or expecting others to free us, to give us the permission to be ourselves. In other words, our life is still lived with the underlying fear that we cannot consistently live in truth.

In this penultimate step, we revisit the process of how our conditioned responses have often come to define our experience of ourselves. While we eventually become initiated into the ways of existing in the world while growing up, learning to lie in order to survive, we usually express our truth freely as children. As we grow, we find that there are people who will not accept this truth, who may, in fact, shame us for being truthful. We begin the habit of protecting ourselves in order to save ourselves from being hurt, from not being able to be who we are. The patterns we develop in order to avoid pain become part of our conditioning. We move in the world with this conditioning, pretending it is the truth of who we are. We also begin the constant search to find sanctuaries, places where we can be who we are freely without condemnation. We look for cherished situations or people, cherished because they seem so rare, where we feel that we are truly safe to appear. But since these opportunities are based on another person or a set of circumstances, they are still external, conditional forces. We still need the circumstances to be right for us to shine.

In Truth of Beauty terms, when we own our lives, our purpose becomes the sanctuary we are looking for. We can't be outside of safety anymore, because in Own our entire definition of what it means to be safe changes. If we are faithful to who we know ourselves to be, every circumstance is the right circumstance to appear.

In Appear, we are determined to bring our beautiful selves to every situation, and when we feel unable to, we explore why we are still giving any person or experience power over us. In Own, instead of the familiar paradigm of entering situations or relationships trying to determine how much of our truth we must withhold in order to avoid experiencing pain, we stand in our truth 100% and know that the only pain that can harm us now is being unfaithful to ourselves.

When we Own, we believe with conviction that no person or conditioned response can remove us from the experience of our beauty. This doesn't mean that we don't experience challenges from time to time. It means that when we experience a loss of power, or what feels

*It is our deepest confrontation
with self that illuminates
our path to beauty.*

like an invitation for our beauty to be diminished, we stand fully present. If being beautiful is uncomfortable, then we watch ourselves feel uncomfortable. But what we can no longer do is apologize for who we are or retreat from expressing our truth.

In Appear, we may be tempted from time to time to ride the train of "Look what they did to me"; in Own, those train tracks are blown up for good. There are no victims in Own, only survivors. We are not responsible for others' bad behavior. What we are responsible for is our decision about their behavior and how that influences our own choices and actions. We take full responsibility for our lives, which is also what it means to become an adult.

Own completes our process of surrender to our three words. Until we reach the stage of Own, much of our experience of life is about manipulation. Therefore, we go into crisis. When you no longer need to control to get what you want, what is false about you begins to shed. This includes the agreements that we make, and the people and things we have attracted into our lives based on our limiting knowledge of self.

Fear requires us to constantly control; when we are not in our truth we are afraid that one day we will be called out as frauds. We look at our lives and say, "This isn't who I am, this isn't the relationship I want, this isn't what I visualize for myself." We discover that much of what we have created was in reaction to our defenses, to our history; and that we haven't made the choice to be our beautiful selves, living the beautiful life that only we know.

Own invites us to experience a radical shift in consciousness. Often our circumstances will follow. What is false begins to slip away. Some clients see reaching this step as having to start over, as opposed to a wonderful opportunity and adventure that leads us deeper into self. Some get angry. Particularly with toxic or unhealthy relationships that begin to change, there may even be a feeling of sadness, betrayal or confusion. They ask, Why does owning my own life mean that another part of my life has to end?

A good friend of mine, Diego, reached out to me during a break in his busy work schedule and asked if we could meet. I was delighted to discover he was back in New York having completed a recent project, yet I sensed some anxiety over the phone. I told him I'd be very happy to see him that afternoon and we decided on a place and time to meet.

Diego is an up-and-coming filmmaker who has enjoyed some recent success and recognition with his work. He had taken an interest in the Truth of Beauty process and I was coaching him through the steps. When I reached the restaurant, I complimented him on his dark designer suit, and noticed his black hair was longer than I remembered. He'd even taken my suggestion to grow a full beard. While I sensed a new confidence with his physical appearance, the step of Appear had been a major turning-point for him and the way he felt about himself on the inside. He'd found consistently appearing in his life difficult, and an even greater challenge arose when we began to discuss what it meant to Own.

When we sat down to talk, despite his warm, open smile, I could see that Diego was very upset. He ran his fingers through his dark hair and said, "I'm not sure where to start. It's my good friend, Andrew. I told you about him before, I think. He's a playwright, but he works as a college administrator. We met in an acting class, and we've been like brothers to each other since I moved to New York. I love him, even though we haven't spoken in over six months now."

When I asked Diego if his concern was that his friendship with Andrew was over, he replied, "We've had periods where we haven't spoken before, minor disagreements that lasted a few days or weeks. Somehow this feels different. So, I guess the honest answer to your question would have to be I'm not sure."

"What happened exactly?"

"It was right around the time I found out that I'd gotten a grant I'd applied for. It wasn't a million dollars, but the money made a big difference for a film I've been working on. Andrew had been so supportive until then, we've always encouraged each other's endeavors. He's made some great observations about my films in editing, and I've read several drafts of his plays. We've talked of collaborating one day.

"Then right after I found out about the grant, I called him with some other big news. I got a call from someone who offered to represent me – this person represents very successful artists that we both admire. I called Andrew right away, and he seemed excited but a little distant, I assumed maybe he was tired. Then he texted me back the next day and told me he didn't think I should go with the agent, that if I did I'd be making a big mistake.

"I couldn't believe his response. Suddenly he was talking about what it meant to be a 'real artist' versus a 'hack'. He named artists we both admire who, in his opinion, have become hacks, who had 'wasted their talent', and he said he worried that would happen to me. I told Andrew that this man's contacts could be very helpful, that it could lead to a chance one day to direct a major Hollywood film. Suddenly, he was shouting at me. That began a long argument, and while he didn't use the word, I felt that he was calling me a 'sell-out'. When I confronted him about it, he said I misunderstood what he meant. But then we had a conversation a few days later and he basically said the same thing – how I've gotten out of touch with my vision and my connection to what is real in my work. Before I said something I regretted, I found an excuse to get off the phone with him. We haven't spoken since."

"Have you tried to reach out to him?"

There was an extended silence before Diego spoke again. He looked at me with what could have been read as hostility but was clearly pain and resignation. "No, I haven't. Why should I?"

"Why shouldn't you?"

"Because, to tell you the truth, I don't want to. In the past when we've argued, we've both apologized later. But this felt like a complete ambush. I have no idea where any of it is coming from. If that's what he thinks about me, I'm not sure I'm interested in his friendship anymore."

Diego acknowledged that, while he genuinely feared the friendship was over, he also felt a sense of relief. Andrew had been critical of him too often – like Diego's father, who had wanted him to be a doctor and who also had very specific ideas of what success looked like. Diego had never admitted to Andrew, or his father, that these definitions of who he should be felt confining and oppressive.

Because Andrew had not achieved any material success with his work, nor had a play produced, Diego felt that it was easier for Andrew to maintain his artistic purity and standards – they had never been challenged. Andrew, who had stopped writing completely, had been very supportive of Diego's projects at first, but Diego began to suspect that there was a growing resentment between them. Whenever he would encourage Andrew to return to his own work, Andrew would claim to be doing "research" for some new idea and then change the subject.

Diego paused briefly, and sighed. "To tell you the truth, I'm so tired of this story. I've told it so many times and repeated it over and over in my head. It's exhausting."

I translated what Diego said in Truth of Beauty terms. "Good. This means you are tired of listening to your conditioning. That's a great place to be. You want to be exhausted with the part of your story that remains stuck in your conditioning. If you're bored, then you might consider that there's another story out there, one that works better for you. Until you grow tired of it, you won't transform it."

"I know my frustration about not being seen in my life doesn't begin with Andrew," Diego admitted. "I've been here before. Many times. I guess this is part of the work, acknowledging that what I'm experiencing didn't begin with him."

"Exactly."

In the last year, perhaps more than ever before in his life, Diego had been consistently appearing. We had begun with the first step of Trust and had spoken briefly about how much he loved having conversations about politics with his grandfather before he died. It was a memory that always restored his confidence in himself and moved him deeply. He had shared with me the concept of Liberation, a very important theme in his life, as his first word. His second word, Discipline, which he often feared he lacked, had been a tool in getting deeper into his work, finishing up projects that had been abandoned at various stages. His third word, Awareness, meant that he was entirely focused on the people that he interviewed for his films, and gave his subjects and his work the concentration they deserved.

Diego allowed me to share what I interpreted occurred with Andrew. I reassured Diego that we were not judging Andrew at all. But what I could say with confidence was that I felt that they had reached different places in their process; or rather, Diego had come to a point where, in order to Appear, he knew he couldn't hold anyone else responsible for his relationship to his creativity. His relationship to his work and his life had changed entirely when he reached this step. Own meant that going forward, he would consistently take responsibility for his experience in the world. That wasn't an indictment of his friendship, or of Andrew; it was the truth about his relationship to responsibility and power.

"Diego, I know this is painful for you, but you didn't abandon Andrew any more than you abandoned your father when you decided not to be a doctor and to become a filmmaker. Given the belief systems you and Andrew shared, there may have been an inevitability to this confrontation. It isn't about either of you being 'right' or 'wrong', it's about your relationship to your truth. When you made the decision – and it is a decision – to own your life, which means owning the way that you think and express yourself in the world, there was no way you could stay in a relationship of victimization around your art. Give Andrew time. Because Andrew has a purpose and a path, just as you do, he may have some fresh insight on what has happened in the relationship. Remember your first word, Liberation. You have liberated yourself to new levels in your work and you want the same for Andrew. But loving him also means accepting where he is right now in his consciousness."

I am grateful for the experience of coaching Diego because it helped me understand a piece critical to the concept of Own: for some of us, owning our lives can feel like we are betraying someone else. While working with Diego, I often had to remind him that his decision not to be a doctor, as his father wanted, wasn't the equivalent of raiding his father's bank account and taking the stolen money as his own. He intellectually knew what I was saying, and said the analogy was perfect. Whenever he chose himself, he felt he was stealing.

Feeling we are betraying someone else when we choose to own ourselves is not uncommon. To own is seen as a selfish act – and it is! But not selfish in the usual meaning of the word. It isn't greedy to insist on being all that we are. But if we have had it presented to us, especially from an early age, that to be fully ourselves means that we are diminishing or taking from someone else, the step of Own might feel excruciating.

We have to be brave enough to explore where these thoughts come from and to allow the grief to come up as we ask: When did I learn that being myself meant someone else was unable to be themselves, or fulfilled in their life?

We are not here to be someone else's reason for living; we don't have that kind of power. Own is deeply personal and private. It belongs to you. One life per person. Diego realized that owning his life and his art wasn't about diminishing anyone else's, but a celebration of himself; he was able to be generous to Andrew, his father, and most importantly, to himself.

The step of Own is the point in your story where truth is now beginning to guide you, not your conditioning. In Own, truth isn't a place we visit like a vacation at Disneyland, or where we have a summer home. It's not a stop on a tour where we get out of the car, take a few pictures and then get back on the same old road we've travelled. With Own, this is where we live. And if for some reason you choose to abandon that truth, you don't course-correct by waiting for someone else to tell you what your truth is. Your goal is to stay constantly aware, constantly vigilant and in the present moment in every situation. If you are in Own, you are always asking yourself, Am I in my truth in this moment, and if I'm not, why not? You are the only one to ask, and you are the only one to answer.

In other words, Own requires us to take a daily inventory of our choices, to challenge ourselves whenever we find we are engaging in what I often refer to as CDB: Complain, Defend, Blame. As soon as we sense we are in CDB on any level, we immediate choose to shift our perspective. If there is nothing standing between you and yourself, if there is no one to blame, if there is no one to fix, if your relationship to your power isn't disabled because of something someone said or did to you, if you don't have to go back into history to change what happened, or manipulate someone in the present to get what you want, if, in fact, you move out of manipulation and control completely, if the only voice you hear when you turn down the conditioning is your own, then your experience of your creativity, your beauty and your life is entirely on you.

You are never alone when you are home within yourself. And, in many ways, by taking responsibility for yourself, you are supporting people with whom you are in relationship.

Consider the implications if we all lived this way, if everyone took responsibility for themselves. Society is there for us, but only as we are there for society. You serve others by being in your truth. You give people what they really need by giving it to yourself first. This is the true power of transformation. Committing to your purpose in life is your gift to yourself, and everyone around you inherits the glory. When you give yourself permission to stand firmly in your life, you inspire others to stand firmly in their own.

As you work through the step of Own, be patient with the part of yourself that holds on to thinking there is some payoff in feeling guilt and shame. But when you truly know, not just as an intellectual idea but in your soul, that going back into those limitations won't get you what you want, then the only way you can move is forward. When you are committed to truth there are no other roads. Living your beauty all the time – full on, without apology or regret – that is the meaning of owning your truth.

In Appear, you learned how to show up for the situations that challenge you by practicing acceptance. In Own, we appear without question. Life is no longer a practice drill, and dress rehearsals are over. Whatever the circumstance, you insist on appearing now. Whatever you think you need to show up today, you have in your possession. The only thing standing between you and your beautiful life – that can ever stand in your way – is the belief that you don't deserve to have one.

Own is hands-on, nothing to contemplate, nothing to negotiate. We have to get our feet wet. What we know to be true on the inside is reflected more than ever before in the outer manifestation of ourselves. This is the beginning of what it means to be fully realized in the world.

Own is practical. You're allowed to get it wrong in Own – believe me, I know firsthand how challenging it is – but you can't think your way out of Own. The only way to get Own wrong is not to risk ourselves in the world. We must take a chance on revealing who we are.

Own can be difficult because it leaves you fully exposed. There are no hiding places in Own. The good news is that, when you begin to drop all the myriad ways you've created to protect yourself, you will find that you have new energy. The energy that you have used, as Caroline Myss writes, "to finance your history" is available in ways you've never experienced before. It is energy that can be used in the present moment; energy to create the life you want. You may find that dreams begin to come true. Your relationship to synchronicity changes. Your intuition improves. Many of my clients notice they look and feel younger, as if weight had dropped from their spirit. In this new space, what you imagine is possible for yourself may change. Surprises await. A client of mine woke up one morning and decided she needed to travel alone for two months overseas, and she hadn't even thought of this type of adventure before. With Own, the conviction of our commitment to truth quiets down our conditioning enough that we can finally hear the sound of our own voice. Your soul tells you what you need, and perhaps for the first time, you can finally hear what it wants. Unlike the radio station that you hear between towns on a road trip – clear for a while and then vaguer as you travel on – this station never goes out of range. In own, we are attuned to the frequency of our spirit and we see that flow manifest in our lives.

Our ability to create also changes. Trust is no longer an exercise to return you to a relationship with self, it is your state of being. Now that you trust yourself again, you may start to ask, perhaps for the first time and from the deepest soul level: What do I want to express in the world? What does my beautiful self really look like? When you know that you own the space you are in the world, and are not just renting, the garden you plant in your yard is different.

When you give yourself permission to stand firmly in your life, you inspire others to stand firmly in their own.

Some of my clients experience this step, like each of the steps, as a momentary crisis. They find they have more fear as "themselves" than when they were controlled by their conditioning. It can be a little scary; as though you've been an imposter in your own story. If you haven't been living your life fully before, then who has? But the newness you now feel is that you are fully integrated for the first time. In Own, you not only own your conditioning, you own all of your experiences. Nothing exists outside of your circle of truth.

Remember: Own is an opportunity, a new place in your life to enter. In Own, you come to discover that owning your truth means having complete authority and responsibility for your beauty. Responsibility is never the same as being controlling. The choice to be controlling is rigid, keeps us bound, and requires us to be hyper-aware of everyone else, terrified of what we may or may not know. When you are in control you have to constantly assess situations so that you can stay in control. This is exhausting and uses up most of your creative power.

When you are responsible, however, you have a sense of obligation to yourself and to the world. You say to yourself, "No matter what comes my way, I have a process now for how I am going to respond to my experiences. I allow life to guide me, offering solutions to which I choose to respond without fear, appearing fully in each moment as who I know myself to be. I may get it right sometimes with my conditioning, I may get it wrong, but two things are always certain: 1) I know that I am always beautiful when I choose to be responsible. I don't get to blame others, and I don't get to blame myself either. Blame is never transformative – responsibility is; and 2) I know that my objective, my only objective, is to find the beauty in everything, and because I have now developed a relationship with myself, I know that if I am not having a beautiful experience, I need to check in with me, first and last. Trying to change or manipulate someone to get the experience I want just isn't a consideration anymore."

When your conditioning arrives to challenge you, as it often does ferociously when you decide to own your life, you don't get to put anyone in between you and your conditioning – not your parents, not your boss, not your best friend. Wherever you think the conditioning came from, whoever "gave" it to you in the beginning, it is essential to realize that it is all yours now – you own it. We can't appear in the world when our power requires us to ask for a vote by committee. How can you see your reflection in the mirror with a crowd of people standing in front of you? You can't own what you can't even see. When you are living a life ruled by your conditioning, being in the world can feel like you are facing a hostile mob. When you choose to live in Own, you are an individual, choosing to exist within a community.

Isn't it wonderful finally to have confirmed what you've always suspected? There is no circumstance or person to wait for to be fully radiant, to live fully in your magnificence.

Commit

Beauty begins when we end the war with self. In the final Truth of Beauty step, Commit, we commit to all we have learned and embrace this truth as our new path. In Commit, owning our lives becomes not just a step in the right direction, but a daily practice we commit to for the rest of our lives.

We have come to understand that in a beautiful life there are no hiding places. We are fully exposed for who we are – something to be celebrated. We appreciate that our beauty has never been dependent on someone else's approval, the circumstances we find ourselves in, or a million other reasons for why we are unable to live our truth. When all of this is stripped away, we are left with what is most essential. We are left with ourselves.

To commit to living beautifully means that the entirety of who you are is available to you at all times. You step into the world each day from a place of wholeness. You know yourself to be complete. You can identify your insecure thoughts for what they are – part of your conditioning. But unlike the past, you now choose to see your conditioning as an opportunity that allows you to continue to unveil your deepest truth. You welcome these opportunities to reveal more of who you are.

You recognize that in any moment when you appear as you know yourself to be, you are beautiful. This sometimes means facing the unknown or unfamiliar. But we face the future and our commitment head on because we now know we have no other option. We are ruthless in this pursuit, but it is the right kind of ruthlessness. We cut off all avenues to other choices. It's beauty through truth or nothing. And when we aren't having a beautiful experience, we know we have the power and the tools to find out why. If we are feeling disconnected from our experience, we know that we can't look to the world to change our mind. We have to go within. This perception is no longer an extravagant thought, as it may have been when we began this journey. The idea of constantly maintaining our connection to purpose becomes as habitual in our lives as showering or deciding what to eat for breakfast. Own is a decision we make about our relationship to our lives. Commit is our dedication to that way of life.

We can chase illusions, of course, we can play games, for years or decades if we choose, but our knowledge of the path to beauty is so powerful now that even our lies will eventually return us to the inevitable experience of our truth. So why not save time, commit to your purpose and do what you came here to do!

The decision to live a beautiful life means living at the highest altitude. It is the major turning-point, and for some, one of life's scariest realizations, when you finally acknowledge that you are 100% responsible for your beauty. This puts you completely at the center of your existence. There is no protection necessary, no separation anymore between you and your experience of being beautiful. We may ask ourselves, "What will happen if I fail?" But there is no failure when we commit, only when we try to live our lives separated from our truth.

When we know we have a right to exist, we forge a bond with the innate part of ourselves that always guides us. We may not listen every single time our truth speaks to us, but we can feel that it is always trying to move us, like an internal compass, towards who we know ourselves to be.

That is why Commit is deeper than an intellectual understanding. Your knowledge of who you are touches your soul and has an impact on every part of your experience. The fragmented life is over. You begin to see that an unwavering commitment to you also means commitment to all of society. You realize that all things are interconnected and that how you are in the world is how the world is in return. There is no divide, no separation. As you show up for the world fully the world shows up for you.

Commit is achieved through practice; asking throughout the day, again and again, Who am I being right now, in this moment? And in this moment. And in the next. Am I being the person I truly know myself to be, no matter what circumstance I find myself in, versus the conditioned self I was taught to construct? This becomes the real challenge; can I be beautiful right here, right now, regardless of the circumstances, and if not, why? In order to be fully in Commit, we must make the decision once and for all to fall out of love with our conditioning, which is often the only experience of love we know.

The decision to finally face our conditioning is swimming in the deep end, in the water past the safety ropes. It is one of the requirements for lasting change. We examine our conditioning; we look it straight in the eye. We don't judge, but we appreciate where it comes from, knowing that ultimately we must let go of our dependency and reliance on it. We may never be rid of it completely, but we want to reach a point in our relationship to self where it doesn't make our decisions for us. We may feel that the part of us that has never stopped being a child has finally grown up. If we are a parent, we are also given a chance to teach our children to follow their truth early, so that they become adults who innately live a beautiful life.

The eighth step, Commit, which completes the Truth of Beauty process, is not an ending, but a beginning. We open our minds to greater awareness. My Truth of Beauty work continues daily with my family, friends and clients. You have gone through each step, read each chapter, and you can see a new you on the horizon. And while you may not live there consistently yet, you have envisioned what may not have felt possible before: the potential of living life openly as you are without fear. For some of us, this may be the first experience of living with the mask off, not unlike an artist lifting the sheet off a new sculpture, unveiling it before the world. How will we be received? In some ways, it seems as if the work is finished, when in reality, the most creative part of our journey has just begun.

Commit is your personal truth in action. When we are committed to truth, we enter any situation with boldness. We have new coordinates. When trauma leads us, we are permanently stuck at the negotiating table: Show me a world that is safe, then I'll appear. But the irony is, *the only way to feel safe in life is to appear.* Safety is being yourself; the only safety you can count on is the commitment you make to knowing yourself. That's what every page of this book has been about.

Sometimes, I'll admit, it is painful to stand unflinchingly in our beauty, and see who comes to our party. There are some who may choose to leave. The results of living from truth will definitely astound you, be prepared. But in commitment, we are not afraid to look, to test our lives in the outside world against our truth, and then see what happens. Having relationships with others and being in the world are the only way to affirm how deep our commitment is. Anyone can feel powerful sitting in a brand-new car in the driveway; this is a show you must take on the road.

True beauty is a contact sport. There are no sidelines; you are going to get dirty from time to time because that is the only way to learn. When a client reaches the step of Commit, we establish an understanding with each other. Whatever happens in our session, one thing is assured; we will no longer blame other people. For some of us, speaking from a place where we no longer blame is like learning a foreign language. I tell my clients clearly; I will no longer engage with you on that level, it is too far removed. Blame began to die a death once we practiced Acceptance. Remember, we don't want validation from the world, we want confirmation; confirmation of who we already know ourselves to be.

It is an old adage, and it's hung around because it is true: old habits die hard. Perhaps the most challenging aspect of Commit is that once you know the truth, and you are faced with a difficult situation, you have to walk through it. There are no short cuts. We get frustrated with the process because we think we've been ourselves our entire lives; but we may have only been ourselves, our authentic selves, for about five minutes. We have to be patient, knowing that if we are committed, we will see results.

No one wakes up with the intention of being unhappy in the world. We all want to shine. Everyone I work with, without exception, is looking for a way to express themselves fully, to expand, to feel powerful, and live as their best, most beautiful self. But we learn from an early age to force our way through, to pretend to know what we are doing, to wear a mask. We all know there are situations where a good mask comes in handy, but eventually all masks fall off, and what is true remains. Wouldn't it be easier to drop the mask now and approach what is true, now?

When we know we have a right
to exist, we forge a bond with
the innate part of ourselves
that always guides us.

A client of mine once described the final step of Commit as the feeling of quiet after a long and tumultuous storm. What she felt, she said, was something she'd never quite felt before, a sense of peace in her soul. She didn't have to fight anymore just to be. She found she was still walking the same streets every day, still dealing with the same people, but with a completely different state of mind. When you are in total awareness of who you are, life simply cannot remain the same.

The one thing we all have in common is a longing to be whole. As you commit to beauty and find your life healing, you may also observe that there are friends, family and partners who are still in great pain. Living from a place of real integration can be challenging. Too many people in the world are fragmented and torn, they feel the division in their lives, and they don't know they can't run from it or solve it by fixing other people. Eventually the separation gets worse, and then they get angry. It is okay to accept the people in our lives who are struggling to appear, who may be angry, and still choose to appear ourselves.

The negotiation of self always leads to anger. No one likes to fight for their life, and if you aren't 100% committed to your truth, somewhere in your life you are at war. Anger is one of the easiest ways to respond when we feel fear or hopelessness. We are frustrated, using the wrong tools to get ourselves out of our pain, digging ourselves in deeper. We battle with "them", we battle with ourselves, we battle with our thoughts, and all of this internal and external noise lets us off the hook from having the real conversation we need to have, from asking the only question that will lead to lasting change: What is my purpose? Who am I and who do I envision myself to be in this moment? Can I participate in the world based solely on my truth, and if not, why?

A client asked me recently if there was ever a time when anger could be productive or justified. She was concerned that the idea of not being angry was very close to the conditioning that she had received as a child – good girls don't get angry. I clarified an important difference between anger that keeps us stuck and powerless, rooted in blame and non-transformative, and the kind of anger that transforms.

She was speaking about the desire for change in the world. Our lengthy conversation led us to a consideration of the iconic civil-rights activist Rosa Parks. While I would never presume to know what Rosa Parks felt on the day she refused to give up her seat on a segregated Mississippi bus in 1955 – an act of insurrection that gave energy and life to help mobilize an entire movement – I did ask my client to consider the photographic images of Parks. Rosa Parks may have been very angry about what was happening to her, but what

I observed in the images was a stillness, a knowing, a depth; Parks, in resisting the order to go to the back of the bus, was beautiful. Shouting and kicking while being arrested may have gotten her some results, but it is my belief that the quiet power that emanated from her as she was led from the bus and off to jail was louder than any scream. Parks, as we know, wasn't the first person to resist Jim Crow laws in the South and she wouldn't be the last; but there was something deeply persuasive in her act of resistance. There may have been anger, but there was also an unquestioning commitment to truth, purpose, and her desire to appear. The entire movement was infused with this beautiful energy. What we know is that she existed within a society that, in part, wasn't inviting her to appear; some people didn't even acknowledge her as an equal citizen. She didn't have to agree with this, but she did have to accept it, staring it in the face before she could consider transforming it. What is compelling about Parks is that her commitment to appear was unwavering, despite all the ugliness around her. Her actions were based on truth, which is why she continues to inspire. She is a testament to the fact that the world does not have to be as beautiful as we would like for us to take a beautiful stand, to pour our beauty into it. When we commit fully, we become the hero of our story, we are the champion of our lives.

What the world needs now, more than anything else, are people who know who they are. Those who choose to stand completely in their beauty, who have been courageous enough, committed enough to seek the truth, to move deeper into self, and who are able to face their conditioning, and to say, despite great fear: This is my purpose and I will enact it in the world, regardless. I know exactly why I am here – to share my truth. There is so much blame and finger-pointing in the world, so much rage at each other, but what we are missing are people who go out into the world committed to sharing their beauty without expectations or prerequisites; who can stand and say, "This is who I am, I know that I am beautiful" – people who not only say the words but who embody them, people who "walk the runway" of life every day.

You know these people. You've passed them on the street and wondered what that special quality was, the inner radiance that mesmerized you. Maybe you have felt that radiance from time to time within yourself. The Truth of Beauty path has been about providing you the tools so that you can locate the place in you that is committed to joy. And when you stand in your power, you illuminate the path to beauty for others.

Leading a purposeful life doesn't mean that we have to smile all the time. We can cry, we can grieve, we can even have an impossible day when we want to go right back to bed. The difference is that by choosing to live from purpose, we no longer abandon ourselves and we don't disappear in order to survive. We stand fully in our circumstances. And we have faith that in each and every moment, a beautiful choice is always available to us. It seems like such a simple thing, but actually it is quite extraordinary when you achieve it; the decision to exist in the world fully as yourself, the ability simply to be.

With trust in yourself, anything is possible. Vulnerability becomes your strength, your permission to play, to laugh, to love, and to express your natural radiance. On this new journey, your ticket is paid for, the baggage is light. Imagination now becomes illumination, restoring your power to create. You now have everything you've ever needed for beauty and all you'll ever need. The search for completion is over. You're the one you've been waiting for.

Now step outside. Your beautiful world awaits you.

CPSIA information can be obtained
at www.ICGtesting.com
Printed in the USA
BVHW071033251121
622518BV00013B/432/J